Jean.

with love from Ted.

July 1965.

SWARTHMORE LECTURE 1965

THE SWARTHMORE LECTURES

SWARTHMORE LECTURE 1965

SEARCH FOR
REALITY IN RELIGION

BY

JOHN MACMURRAY

LONDON

GEORGE ALLEN & UNWIN LTD
MUSEUM STREET

PRINTED IN GREAT BRITAIN
in 11pt Baskerville type
BY HEADLEY BROTHERS LTD
109 KINGSWAY LONDON WC2
AND ASHFORD KENT

PREFACE

The Swarthmore Lectureship was established by the Woodbrooke Extension Committee at a meeting held December 7th, 1907; the minute of the Committee providing for "an annual lecture on some subject relating to the message and work of the Society of Friends". The name "Swarthmore" was chosen in memory of the home of Margaret Fox, which was always open to the earnest seeker after Truth, and from which loving words of sympathy and substantial material help were sent to fellow-workers.

The Lectureship has a twofold purpose; first, to interpret further to the members of the Society of Friends their Message and Mission; and, secondly, to bring before the public the spirit, the aims and the fundamental principles of Friends. The Lecturer alone is responsible for any opinions expressed.

The Lectures have usually been delivered at the time of the assembly of London Yearly Meeting of the Society of Friends. The present Lecture, in abridged form, was delivered at Friends House, Euston Road, on the evening of May 21st, 1965.

A list of previous Lectures, as published in book form since 1940, will be found at the beginning of this volume, and those prior to 1940 at the end.

BIOGRAPHICAL NOTE

JOHN MACMURRAY. Born at Maxwellton, Kirkcud-
bright. Educated at the Grammar School and Robert
Gordon's College, Aberdeen; Glasgow University
where he received his M.A. and LL.D., and Balliol
College, Oxford, where he received an M.A. He
served with the army in France during the First
World War, first with the R.A.M.C. and later as a
lieutenant with the Queen's Own Cameron Highlanders when he was awarded a Military Cross. After
the war he lectured in Philosophy at Manchester
University, 1918-19, was Professor of Philosophy at
the University of Witwatersrand, Johannesburg,
1919-21; Fellow and Tutor of Balliol College, Oxford,
from 1921 to 1928; Professor of Philosophy, London
University College, 1928-44; Professor of Moral Philosophy, Edinburgh University, 1944-57. Professor
Macmurray was a member of the Inter-University
Council for Higher Education Overseas from its foundation until 1957. He has travelled extensively in the
U.S.A. and has visited Jamaica, Ghana and Nigeria.

Publications:

  Freedom in the Modern World (Faber, 1932).
  Interpreting the Universe (Faber, 1933).
  Philosophy of Communism (Faber, 1933).
  Creative Society (Faber, 1935).
  Reason and Emotion (Faber, 1935).
  Structure of Religious Experience (Faber, 1936).
  The Clue to History (S.C.M. Press, 1938).
  The Boundaries of Science (Faber, 1939).
  Challenge to the Churches (Faber, 1941).
  Constructive Democracy (Faber, 1943).
  Conditions of Freedom (Faber, 1949).
  The Self as Agent (Faber, 1957).
  Persons in Relation (Faber, 1961).
  Science, Art and Religion (University of Liverpool
    Press, 1961).

CONTENTS

PRELUDE—PURPOSE AND METHOD

WHEN I was invited to prepare the Swarthmore Lecture for 1965 I felt grateful for the invitation and bound to accept it. When I came to consider what its theme should be I found myself in a difficulty. It was only recently that I had been accepted into membership of the Society of Friends. Yet I felt that I should try to speak to the condition of the Society as a member of it. I could not speak from a maturity of Quaker experience. I am still only beginning to discover the meaning of my commitment to the Society, and am not yet fully absorbed into its life and its purpose. My religious experience and my thoughts about religion have been formed outside the Society, and at the age of seventy-four they are apt to be fully formed and very difficult to alter.

On reflection, it seemed to me that I could serve this occasion best by setting myself to understand the processes and the pressures which led me, at the end of my public life, to seek the fellowship of the Society of Friends. In a real sense, this was the conclusion of a lifetime of religious reflection, which had been itself a search for reality in religion. I have never been much interested in my own past; and in the past at all I have been interested only for the light that it throws on the present and the future. So the task I set myself was an unfamiliar one, and rather uncongenial. But I found it rewarding, and what I have to offer you now is the result of it. In particular, I found that my religious reflection had tended to concentrate not on religion as it has been or is now, but upon its future—

upon what it can be and will be. And I discovered that it was my beliefs about that future which led me, more than anything else, to the desire to become a Quaker. So I chose, as the title and theme of my lecture, "Search for Reality in Religion".

By training and by professional experience I am, I suppose, an intellectual. I have taught philosophy in universities in Manchester, Johannesburg, Oxford, London and Edinburgh. Apart from teaching I have carried on a continuity of philosophical thinking which has led me to conclusions of my own, some of which I shall have occasion to mention later. A philosopher is necessarily involved in a commitment which has itself a religious quality. He is dedicated to reason in the pursuit of truth, whatever the consequences to himself or his society, and whatever its effects upon his own beliefs and prejudices and on those of his fellows. The effort to live up to this ideal soon becomes a habit in those who are committed to it; and nearly everything that I have written has been governed by it. Inevitably this raises the problem of the relation of faith and reason, as a practical, not a theoretical one, unless one is prepared to reject religion. *This* solution I have never even considered. I have, indeed, rejected much that is often considered a part of religion; even a necessary part. I have thought it possible that we do not yet know very clearly what religion properly is. I have sought some means to distinguish false religion so that I might reject that. But to think that religion as such, and in every form, is illusory and pointless has always seemed to me as preposterous as it would be to think the same of music. The view of the relation of faith and reason which I have found most congenial, at least as a working hypothesis, is that of Aquinas. Rational enquiry must start from matter of common fact. It must proceed by its own laws to the limit of its possibilities, in the conviction that though the individual thinker may err, it can only be by thinking badly. Thought itself is a divine gift, to be used and trusted; and truth must, in the end, be *one*, without incoherence or contradiction. In the sphere of faith the procedure must be different, since we start from the beliefs that take us beyond common factual experience, and are in some sense personal revelations. From these we proceed towards the world of common experience where they have their exemplification or their reference. So faith completes reason, and there is a field of knowledge where they meet and overlap, confirming and establishing one another. I would only add that this contrast between faith and reason is a *prima facie* distinction with which we start. In the end we may discover that it is not so clear-cut as it seems. It depends upon limitations we impose and conceptions we define. In the concrete we may discover that faith and reason have more in common than we are inclined to allow, and that their conflict is largely the outcome of our own mistakes.

In this lecture I intend to speak not as a philosopher but as a person to persons, as a Christian to Christians and, so far as my ignorance permits, as a Quaker to Quakers. I do not wish to start an argument but to find my way to an expression of personal belief. I shall not stay to prove what might be proved, since I am not concerned with philosophy now but with religion; not with conclusions of reason but with a confession of

3

faith. I should like, for this purpose, to escape from the limits of mere intellectual formulation, and speak from the whole of my experience. I am not too sanguine of success. After a lifetime of intellectual effort it is perhaps inevitable that anything I say will be "sicklied o'er with the pale cast of thought". For this I would apologize in advance, trusting that you will treat it as an accident of professional habit. What I desire for my lecture is that it should not be a single theme guided to a climax or conclusion, but more like a musical composition, a series of movements, each with its own tone and temper, yet all belonging together, and constituting a unity. In a word I aim at a statement which shall be as fully personal as I can make it. And because of this, the first movement must be somewhat autobiographical.

FIRST MOVEMENT—
AUTOBIOGRAPHICAL

IN this first section I have to consider my own religious development. It seems necessary to do this if my readers are to understand and to evaluate what I have to say in the sequel. For that is the final product of this development, and finds its motive and much of its meaning there. At the same time I should like to cut the autobiographical material down to what is essential to its purpose. I must give some account of the religion in which I was trained as a child, and in my schooldays. Thereafter I can concentrate upon a few critical points at which changes in this early expression of religion were forced upon me. With such a background I can outline, in conclusion, the stage I had reached when I asked to be received into the fellowship of the Society of Friends, and why I was impelled to take this step.

*   *   *   *   *

I was fortunate to be born into a deeply religious family. My parents were at one in a Christian piety which dictated the form of family life and determined its atmosphere. Its earliest component was the traditional Calvinism of the Scottish Church. This is perhaps the most intellectual of the Christian traditions, with the central stress falling upon soundness of doctrine; with the Bible as the inspired book of reference in any dispute. I can remember the incredulous amazement with which, later on, I heard an English scholar distinguish science and religion as the expressions respectively of the intellectual and the emotional aspects of human consciousness. The centre of my own religious upbringing had been instruction in organized correctness of doctrine, coupled with a distrust and suppression of emotion in favour of the revealed truth. With this went a strict morality expressed in rules and prohibitions, which was itself referred to the authority of scripture and was taken for granted as universally binding. So my religious training made me familiar with theology from an early age and encouraged the systematic study of scripture.

This Calvinist tradition was beginning to lose its earlier strictness in the last decade of the nineteenth century, while I was a child. And it was qualified for my parents by the influence of the evangelical movement. But it was never cancelled; and one of my latest memories of my father is of seeing him as an old man in retirement, seated at a writing table, poring over a great volume of Calvin's *Institutes*, with all the other volumes stacked beside him on the table. But the evangelical influence was profound. Shortly after their marriage, my father and mother were both greatly affected by the mission of the American evangelists, Moody and Sankey. This influence did not displace the earlier religious attitude, but it added something that made it more alive, more personal, more forward-looking. It brought a warmth of feeling to the over-intellectual formality of the old Presbyterianism. The family religion became actively concerned with spreading the gospel, and critical of the state of the Church religion round about. It took on a missionary quality. This was not wholly the effect of the American evangelism. As a young man my father had intended, and trained himself, to go as a missionary to China; but his going was postponed by the Boxer movement there; and while he waited his father died and left him with a mother and an ailing sister to support. So his hope was thwarted, while his interest in the missionary enterprise remained. One result of all this was that I grew up with a feeling that I should fulfil the mission which he had been prevented from carrying out. I knew that this would please him above all things, though he was careful never to suggest to me that I should follow in his steps. So when eventually I went to university, it was with the intention of training to be a missionary. Indeed, before I took my first degree, I did offer myself as a candidate for the Chinese mission field, but by that time, I fear, somewhat half-heartedly, and without special qualifications; and I was not accepted. I went to Oxford instead.

A growing dissatisfaction with the Presbyterian churches moved my father to begin a search for a more satisfactory body of Christians with whom we might associate ourselves. This happened when I was about ten years of age. At that time he was transferred from the extreme south-west of Scotland to Aberdeen, at his own request and expense, for the sake of his children's education. He had, in full measure, the old Scottish faith in and reverence for learning. He took the opportunity of this change to join one of the Baptist churches there. Later, on moving residence, he transferred allegiance to another, more evangelical, Baptist church; but on discovering some irregularity in its financial accounts, he left it, and joined a meeting of the Plymouth Brethren. Thereafter we attended their meetings for worship on Sunday morning and an independent evangelistic mission-hall in the evening.

7

When, in 1909, he was transferred to Glasgow, and I matriculated at the University there, he found a group of people who combined both activities—worship in the mode of the Plymouth Brethren and local evangelism.

The first part of the story ends here. The second part is concerned with the modification of this family religion which I had absorbed, and in the first place by the new pressures of university study. Not very long after this began, my father was compelled by ill-health to retire from work, and the family moved to London, leaving me to complete my studies in Glasgow alone. So at this point I must try to sum up what had happened to me in this earlier religious experience and to assess its permanent value and influence.

The most immediate effect was that while still at school, in the revivalist fervour that followed the mission of Torrie and Alexander, I began to take part regularly in evangelistic activities. I formed a group of boys of my own age, who met weekly in each other's houses for Bible study and prayer. I addressed evangelistic meetings, mostly in the open air. I served as assistant evangelist to a tent mission in Aberdeenshire. I spoke occasionally in the meeting for worship. In all this I was earnest, and in the ordinary and superficial sense, sincere. Looking back upon it, however, I think that all this religious activity was second-hand and somewhat priggish. It was the result of the teaching of others, absorbed and elaborated by a quick and busy mind, rather than the expression of a personal religious experience. In spite of its seriousness and conviction, it was religiously unreal. From this I learned, in the end, how easy it is for religious convictions, in spite of the sincerity and passion with which

8

they are entertained and expressed, to be imitative and imaginary, the products of a romantic sentimentality, or the symbols of pressures in oneself which are not themselves religious. At the same time, I found myself unable to question the reality of the religious experience of my parents, even when the forms of its expression, particularly in doctrine and belief, became more and more incredible to me. It was a long time before I was able to draw the full conclusion from this and to make it fundamental, as it must be, to any religious understanding. It is this. The dichotomy which governs religious experience is one between real and unreal. This is not identical with the intellectual distinction between true and false; nor with the aesthetic distinction between what satisfies or does not satisfy our emotions, even if it is related to these. For it is possible for us to have a real religious experience coupled with religious beliefs and practices which are fallacious and undesirable; or to hold sincerely and convincedly to religious beliefs and practices with no reality to sustain them.

This statement, of course, represents a point of view that I could only formulate very much later. If I set it out here it is to indicate my belief that it was already implicit in my earliest experience. As soon as I began serious reflection on my religious position, it began to show itself, and as the years went by it became more and more evident. But if I now return to a fully factual statement, I might say this. I was convinced that religion had its own reality, so firmly that I have never afterwards been able to question it for a moment. This came from the knowledge of the quality of religious life in my parents; and is the most valuable thing that they gave me. Other important things which remained with me were a thorough knowledge of the Bible, both Old and New Testaments; a good grasp of the major principles of traditional Protestant theology, and of the issues which separated the Protestant churches from the Roman church, and some practical experience of religious activities, particularly evangelistic activities, and the ideas and attitudes which underlie them.

Before I go on to record the important religious changes during the second stage of my life—as a student and as a soldier—there is one developing interest of my childhood and schooldays which, though not religious, must be mentioned here, because of the future influence it was to have upon my religious development. This was an early and continuing interest in science. It began, before I had reached my teens, with astronomy. Ball's "Starland" was my textbook, and it came to me as a revelation. It was followed by a strong interest in biology, so that during my schooldays I read every book that I could find on the plant and animal life of the world. If I had had my own way I should have become a scientist. But headmasters and directors of studies were too strong for me, and my father, in spite of his own belief in education, did not feel competent to decide, against the advice of the teachers, between a classical and a modern curriculum. The schoolmasters had their eyes upon bursary competition and university entrance. My director of studies at Glasgow University, convinced of the superiority of a classical education and the crudity of science as an educational instrument, insisted that I should not sacrifice what I had already gained at school. In both cases I fought a successful rearguard action by winning concessions. I was allowed to include science, both at school and at my first university, as an extra subject in a classical course. At school it was chemistry; at the university, geology. The first provided a sound basis for widening private studies which have continued sporadically throughout my life. The latter provided a first-rate training in various branches of science and their practical applications. Geology has the advantage, in spite of the specialization which science requires, that it must use the help and the techniques of other branches of scientific study. My university course included not merely field-work and microscopic examination, but mineralogy, crystallography, palaeontology, as well as geological map-making and laboratory work in the determination of minerals. I was the only arts student in a large class of pure and applied scientists and mining engineers, and it was the only university class in which I carried off the medal. This solid grounding in science and scientific method has been of the greatest possible use to me not only as a philosopher in a country where few philosophers have any direct experience of science but at least as much in the religious field. For the question of the relation between science and religion has been dominant during my lifetime, and has not merely turned large numbers of intelligent people against religion, but issued in unending controversies and apologetics on behalf of one and the other. In these discussions I have been constantly struck by the ignorance displayed on both sides. The more general impression which I carried away from my scientific studies, however, was that science is far easier than any of the humanistic studies and especially than philosophy. This is, I suspect, a major reason for its astonishing success in our time.

With such a background, then, I matriculated at the University of Glasgow in 1909. I set out to take an Honours degree in Classics, with a classical and literary schooling as my basis, with a passionate belief in science and its application, and with a religious outlook upon my own future. It was natural, in such circumstances, that I should at once join the Student Christian Movement; and, since I intended to become a missionary, the Student Volunteer Missionary Union. During my student days the Student Christian Movement was at the height of its influence in the British Universities, and that influence was, I think, almost wholly for good. In these days it was happy in its leadership, and full of a generous ardour in all its doings. It was fully interdenominational in its attitude, without strain or effort. It was sure enough in its religion to laugh at itself. It had broken through the primness and stuffiness and dogmatism of so much of the traditional religion; yet it remained militant in its Christianity—in its belief in unity, in the possibility of winning the world for Christ "in this generation", and in its vision of the need to concentrate upon applying Christianity in every field of human activity, for the salvation of the life of the world. I doubt if the Christian organizations of today have any idea how much they owe to the Student Christian Movement of those days. I do know that it was the major influence from organized Christianity upon my own religious development. I was a faithful member of the Movement from my first term when I joined one of its study groups, until my last term as a student, when I served as president of the Oxford Branch, after having helped, along with some friends who like myself had returned from military service or from prison camps abroad, to reorganize and re-establish it. If I am to sum up what I learned from the S.C.M.—and any summing up must be ludicrously inadequate—I should say that it taught me that religious fellowship could be fun and that there was no branch of creative human effort which could not be integrated with Christianity.

The rest of my religious development, which was gradual and slow, can best be expressed with reference to a few key points which crystallized its various stages. The first of these happened during the first year of my university studies. I had agreed to conduct a Bible Class for young men of my own age, or a little older, at the Glasgow Mission Hall which I attended. I decided that we would study the Epistle of Paul to the Romans. I made this choice because, as I had been taught, the tap root of Christian theology was to be found here. In my classical studies I had been learning techniques for dealing with ancient texts by way of analysis and comparison, which could, if properly used, lay bare their meaning. I decided, in preparation for my class, to apply these methods to the Epistle to the Romans. I knew, of course, the theological use to which the early chapters were put, as sources of central doctrines. But I put these out of my mind so far as possible, and concentrated upon an analysis of the text as if it were new and unknown to me. The result was startling. I discovered, after checking and rechecking my work, that these great doctrines of the Christian faith just were not there.[1] Their attachment to the text of the Epistle depended upon what seemed to me to be a misunderstanding. Two things about it, however, were decisive. The first was that the theology in which I had been trained could not stand up to a scientific scrutiny of the scriptural text from which it claimed to be derived. This did not result in a rejection of theology, far less of religion itself. But it made theology questionable and so destroyed its dogmatic claims. I did reject *dogma*, in the belief that theology required critical analysis and reconstruction. The second decisive result came from the consciousness that I was using scientific tools to test the validity of my religious beliefs. This had the effect of associating science in general with my religious development, and so saved me from the tension between science and religion which drove so many of my contemporaries out of Christian belief altogether. In the scientific field, I thought, one does not throw science overboard because a favourite theory has been shown to be invalid. Why should it be different in religion? Could we not hope that through testing and modification we should arrive at a religion which science need not be ashamed to serve?

The rest of my university career only enlarged and confirmed these conclusions. In 1913 I took my first degree. A little earlier I had won a Snell Exhibition to

[1] This, I remember, is how I put it to myself, perhaps with youthful exaggeration. What I did find there was the exposition not of a doctrine but of an experience which is available to everyone who puts his trust in Christ. It is the experience of being freed from the hopeless and deadly struggle to obey the moral law, in order to enjoy the glorious liberty of the children of God.

Today, the misunderstanding reminds me of the occasion when George Fox, at Derby in 1650, was committed to the House of Correction "as a blasphemer and as a man that had no sin". (*Journal of George Fox*, Chap. III.)

Oxford. In October, 1913, I entered Balliol College, Oxford, as a scholar, and set myself to a two years' course in Greats. But history had other plans. I had a year only to find my way into the Oxford life, to make the acquaintance of Plato and to watch the skirmishes between idealists and realists in philosophy, before the Great War intervened. By October, 1914, I was in the Army Medical Corps, training as a nursing orderly. I returned to Oxford immediately after the Armistice, took my degree examinations for a shortened course in Greats after two terms and a short vacation; and three months later became a lecturer in philosophy in Manchester University. Here then I may sum up the religious development of my student days, before turning to the experience of war. First of all, the combination of the atmosphere of the S.C.M. and the discovery that traditional theology was questionable proved a great deliverance into religious freedom. Gradually it became easier and in the end quite natural to think for myself in religion as in other fields. I came to think that it might be necessary to transform traditional Christianity into something very different, and that it was quite natural that this should be so. Scientific method had something to do with this, and from science I learned not to throw over a current belief until one could replace it by a better one. I had reached the notion of a theology developing by self-criticism. It remained, however, little more than an idea. I had hardly begun to apply it. But I should never again fall into the gross mistake of *identifying* religion with theology or with any system of beliefs. To this I would add that religion remained for me missionary in outlook and function, and that it became more and more definitely non-sectarian and interdenominational. Before my student days were over my personal outlook in religion was fully and finally ecumenical. My only serious limitation of this was a doubt, stemming as much from Scottish history as from any theory, of the Roman Church.

The Great War caught me, as it caught most people, unawares and unprepared. The first issue that faced me was pacifism. I was strongly moved towards it. But I had never seriously considered the question, and in the long run this decided the matter. I felt that I could not suddenly become a pacifist when I was faced with the call to arms, though I had done nothing about it beforehand. Had I been a Quaker then I should have refused to fight, since this would have been part of an abiding witness. I compromised by joining the Medical Corps, and I was in the army by October, 1914. It was 1915 before I went to France. In 1916 I discovered that I was as much part of a fighting organization as if I had been in the firing line. So I accepted a Commission in the Cameron Highlanders without coming home, and joined my battalion on the Somme. I was wounded in the final German attack, in the defence of Arras in 1918, and invalided home, and I was still unfit for service when the armistice was signed in the end of the year. I was allowed to return to Oxford to finish my degree course there; and I was still undischarged from the army when I took my final examinations in the summer of 1919.

I am concerned here only with the effect of the war upon my religious development. In the field of theory, of belief, nothing happened. It was as though such questions had been put into cold storage "for the duration". Religion, however, and therefore religious development is not primarily a matter of beliefs. The beliefs, so far as they are real, are derivative. The real religion from which they are derived, lies in the depths of one's own being; its development is a development of one's personality itself. Through the experience of war I moved a long way towards my own reality. The first, and perhaps the most effective change which the experience of the battlefield worked in me, was the result of becoming familiar with death. In normal civilian life one hardly ever meets death, and when one does, it is heavily disguised. For the combatant soldier it is not an idea; it is a stark, ever-present, unavoidable fact. After I was commissioned I went alone to join my platoon on the Somme. I found the men I was to command in a reserve trench, well behind the front line. It was a quiet evening, and I had walked over half a mile of open ground to reach them. They were having tea; and I joined them in an angle of the trench. I sat with one of them on one side of the corner, a second was sitting at the corner itself, jesting with a third who was just round the corner so that I could hear but not see him. A few minutes after I had sat down we heard the whine of a shell coming towards us. It landed in our trench, just round the corner, and exploded. When the smoke cleared my neighbour and I rushed to the corner to see what had happened. We found the man round the corner dead—almost cut in two by a flying shard. The man at the corner was bleeding profusely. We shouted for stretcher-bearers, and they took him away, but it seemed unlikely that he could live. Of the four of us who had been talking together a moment before, two were left. As my introduction to the life of a fighting man in the trenches, it was, of course, a shock. But very soon that sort of thing was common-place—part of the routine of daily life.

Just outside my post in the front line itself a dead Highlander, in a full kilted uniform, was hung up in the centre of a mass of barbed wire. It was impossible to get at him without a major operation in no man's land. So there he remained, day after day, almost as if he were one of us. No doubt this normal experience of the soldier on active service affects men differently. With me it resulted in a quick and complete acceptance of death, for myself as well as for my comrades. It had seemed a dreaded end, before the war. Now it became an incident in life, and in the result it removed for ever the *fear* of death. This is a tremendous gain in reality; for until we reach it—however we do reach it—we cannot see our life as it really is, and so cannot live it as we should. The fear of death is the symbol in us of all fear; and fear is destructive of reality. It is true that one can gain this familiarity with death and use it falsely. We can say, as so many of my contemporaries did after the war, "Let us eat and drink, for tomorrow we die." But it may just as well lead us to the opposite conclusion. We may feel that life is precious because it is short; and because it may end at any moment we must live so that every day would be a good day to die in, if death should come. Without this knowledge of death, I came to believe, there can be no real knowledge of life and so no discovery of the reality of religion.

In the second place, I should set, as the product of this new experience, the process of gradual disillusionment which I shared with so many of my comrades in arms. We went into war in a blaze of idealism, to save little Belgium and to put an end to war. We discovered, stage by stage, what childish nonsense all this idealism was. We learned that war was simply stupidity, destruction, waste and futility. We became critical, sceptical and sometimes cynical. By the end of it, we knew that war could never achieve what those who chose it expected it to achieve. It was inherently destructive and wasteful—of life, of time, of a thousand possibilities, as well as of the means of life—of homes and all the hard-won machinery of living. It could stop things—like the plans of the Kaiser—but it could construct nothing. I knew enough of history to realize that the great forward steps in human progress had in most cases been the results of warfare—but not the *intended* results; and the major result of the war in which I fought was wholly unintended—the setting up of communism in Russia.

So by the end of the war we soldiers had largely lost faith in the society we had been fighting for. We felt that we had been "led up the garden path" by the powers that be; that our young enthusiasm and trust and ignorance had been played upon by men whose real interest was in their own wealth and power and prestige. We believed that our leaders were either rascals or blind leaders of the blind. Our eyes were opened. I can still remember how I heard the first post-war House of Commons described from inside as a collection of "hard-faced men who looked as though they had done well out of the war". I said to myself, "That's what *we* thought; and it seems we were right." So it came about that with hundreds of thousands of others I came out of the Great War saying, "Never again!"

There is one incident belonging to this war-time

experience to which I must refer, because it had a decisive influence upon my future religious life. I had been a year and a quarter in France before I had leave to go home for a few days. When I found myself, after this long time, again in civilian surroundings and amongst civilians, I was shocked by the change in their attitude of mind. I felt as though an evil spirit had entered into them, a spirit of malice and hatred. Before twenty-four hours had passed I wanted to get back to the trenches, where for all the misery and destruction, the spiritual atmosphere was relatively clean. It was, I think, the ignorant and superstitious hatred of the Germans, and the equally ignorant and unreal glorification of us, in the trenches, as heroes that had this effect. In France we were not heroes, nor expected to be; and we did not hate Germans, at least not the Germans in the trenches opposite. We understood them, and they understood us. We were sharing the same spurious and obscene life, no doubt with the same feelings. They had been dumped into war, no doubt, as we had, so we had a fellow-feeling for our enemies, which showed itself in odd little ways. I remember one night in the front-line, where we had been enjoying a quiet time, with a Saxon regiment opposite. We had been carrying on our war on the principle, "Don't bother us and we won't bother you." On this night a Saxon soldier on patrol slipped over to our trench and dropped a card on us. It read—in English—"Watch out! The Prussians are taking over tomorrow." A gulf had been fixed, it seemed, between ourselves and our friends and acquaintances in civilian life. We had ceased to understand one another. I can remember feeling, as I returned from this short leave—during which, indeed,

I had got married—that now most of the pacifists were in the trenches.

This was in October, 1916. I had not been long back on the Somme battlefield when I was incapacitated by spraining an ankle. I was only three weeks in hospital in England before I was released on sick-leave, and it was some months before I was able to return to France. During this period I was asked to preach, in uniform, in a church in North London. I took the opportunity to advise the church and the Christians in it, to guard against this war-mentality; and to keep themselves, so far as possible, aloof from the quarrel, so that they would be in a position—and of a temper— to undertake their proper task as Christians when the war was over, of reconciliation. The congregation took it badly; I could feel a cold hostility menacing me; and no one spoke to me when the service was over. It was after this service that I decided, on Christian grounds, that I should never, when the war was over, remain or become a member of any Christian church. I kept to this resolve all my life as a university teacher. It was only after my retirement that I applied for membership of the Society of Friends. (But even during the war, though my knowledge of Quakerism was indirect and impersonal, I had made an exception in its favour because of its attitude to war.) I was not, however, tempted to abandon religion. I justified my refusal to join a religious organization to myself—I had no desire to make a parade of it—as a personal Christian protest against a spurious Christianity. I spoke and wrote thereafter in defence of religion and of Christianity; but I thought of the churches as the various national religions of Europe.

When I left the army and my university studies in 1919, it was without any religious attachment, with a suspicion about the validity of theology, and as a confirmed realist. I had shed the idealism of my pre-war outlook. I had gained a purpose in life; for when I said "Never again!" I meant it as a dedication to the elimination of war from human life. Whatever sphere of activity I might find myself involved in—and my hope then was that it might be on the staff of the new "League of Nations"—I intended to use it to this end. When it appeared that I was to spend my life in teaching philosophy, this became the underlying purpose of all my philosophizing. To this task I brought a mind that had become deeply sceptical of the principles underlying the European civilization in which I had been brought up and which had issued in the savage destruction and stupid waste in which I had played my part. Convinced that the source of error must be deeply hidden, I decided, as a rule to guide my search for it, to distrust and question especially those principles of whose truth I should find my elders most unshakably convinced.

So far as concerned religion I was still a convinced Christian with no doubt that the religious issue was the most central and most important of all issues. But I had given up all the churches; I had turned from the past and was looking to the future, believing that Christianity had to be rediscovered and recreated. When I asked myself, as I did, why I had given up the churches, and why so many of my contemporaries had given up religion by identifying it with the churches, the answer I found for myself and for them was that we could no longer believe in their *bona fides*; that they did not mean what they said; so that what they said, even if it were true, had become irrelevant. I still consider that this is what stands between the world and the church—this question of bad faith—and not intellectual difficulties about out-dated myths or cosmologies. The difficulties are no longer intellectual or theoretical at all. They are *moral*. For very many of my generation, and for even more of the younger generations that have followed us—there hangs about the official representative of religion an odour, not of sanctity, but of disingenuousness. This feeling may be false. But it can only be proved false, I imagine, by a dramatic action that demonstrates its falsity in a manner which cannot be gainsaid or ignored.

With the completion of my Oxford course and my subsequent demobilization, the purpose of this auto-biographical section is complete. One of my reasons for undertaking it was the hope that it might be seen as typical of the process which has taken such a large percentage of the intelligent youth of Europe since the beginning of the Great War outside the influence of religion. The difference in my case was that the process was carried through within an unquestionable conviction that whatever might be true about the traditional Christianity in which I had been trained, religion itself is not merely valid, but central in human life. Consequently my personal development resulted in a deep scepticism of all the traditional expressions of religion, and so brought me down to the bedrock of a belief in the reality of religious experience; indeed in the validity of Christianity, whatever Christianity might really be. It left everything else doubtful. The positive phase of my religious development, which has

23

occupied the whole of my maturity and is still incomplete, has been an effort to discover the *reality* of religion, by answering the question, "What is Christianity?" It was only many years later, when the main lines of my answer had been laid down, that I discovered how closely my own story repeated, a century later, that of Sören Kierkegaard. I might have expressed my own problem in his terms as the problem "How to become a Christian". There were, of course, great differences. How could it be otherwise a century later? As a philosopher I could not see the Hegelian system as the summing up of all philosophy. As a religious seeker, I could not, as he did, take the major doctrines of traditional theology for granted, and as a student of social history I could not accept the radical individualism of his attitude and of his answers. I found myself in these things much closer to the prophetic insight of one of the very greatest of modern thinkers, Martin Buber. But the shape of Kierkegaard's problem and of mine were much the same. For both of us the problem took the form that he taught us to label "existential". There was, however, one occasion which had such a marked effect both in illuminating and enlarging the problem and in redirecting my search for a solution, that it should, perhaps, be included. I was invited to take part in a private conference in London. I found on arrival that my fellow members were representatives of the various Churches for the most part, all of them leaders in their own fields and many of them well known in the country beyond the limits of their own profession. Besides those there were a few men who, like myself, were not churchmen, but laymen with religious interests. What the subject of our conference was to be we did not know until our first meeting, when our host, himself one of the outstanding religious leaders of my generation, suggested that we should discuss the question, "What is Christianity?" We did this for the whole of that day, and in the evening we came to the unanimous conclusion that we did not know. The next day we went on to ask how we could find out; and after a long discussion we concluded that before we could discover what Christianity is we should have to study seriously two other questions. The first of these was the nature of modern Communism, the other was the problem of sex. We then decided that we would tackle Communism first, and appointed one of our number to write a paper about Communism and Christianity which should be the basis of discussion for a later meeting.

It was this conference which led me to undertake a thorough study of the early writings of Karl Marx, with an eye to discovering, in particular, the historical relation between Marxism and the Christian tradition. I was astonished to find how close the relation was and how correct the conviction of the conference was that the study of Communism was a necessary prelude to the understanding of Christianity. I, at least, found that I learned a great deal about Christianity by this study, and especially by coming to understand the reasons behind Marx's rejection of religion. The basic reason was his conviction that religion was the popular, and therefore the important form of idealism[1], and his

[1] *Idealism.* See below pp. 39f; 58ff. and my Essex Hall Lecture, 1944, on *Idealism against Religion.* Wherever the spiritual life is dissociated from the material life, and is valued and pursued for its own sake, we have idealism. The opposite of idealism is the integration of theory and practice, not in theory but in practice. The most obvious expression of idealism in religion is, perhaps, otherworldliness.

rejection of religion was the most serious aspect of his attack upon idealism. My critique of this was so important in my own religious development that I can best complete this section of my lecture by summarizing its conclusion.

I was wholly convinced by Marx that idealism is a dangerous illusion which must be rejected. But I was not convinced that religion is necessarily a form of idealism. In particular, the Hebrew religion, as it appears in the Old Testament, it not idealistic at all. On the other hand, a great deal of what passes for Christianity is undoubtedly idealist, and must either be cured of its idealism or rejected. As this thought developed in my mind I became convinced that idealism and religion are, in the end, incompatible with one another. Their identification by Marx is the basic error of Marxism. Idealist religion is *unreal*. Marx would have been justified in calling for the reform of religion but not for its rejection. Yet this would have led to a wholly different understanding of human society from the communist one. When I looked for the cause of the idealizing of Christianity, I found it in the acceptance by the church of the Roman Empire. This "acceptance" was a long process, though it may seem short by compression when we look back through the centuries. It includes the process by which, under the influence of Greek philosophy, the effort was made to determine an orthodoxy of belief and to extirpate heresy; and equally the process which led to the creation of a hierarchical and authoritarian church parallel to and modelled to some extent upon the organization of the Roman State. The first of these implies a theoretical, or

Greek, conception of Christianity; the second a Roman or legal conception of the Church. The "adoption" of Christianity by Constantine in the early fourth century is a useful date to remember, but, of course, people are not made Christian by the decree of an Emperor. In becoming the religion of the Roman Empire the Church was logically bound to distinguish between the spiritual and the material realms, and to recognize the ordering of the latter as the proper sphere of the State. The function of the Church had to become, in effect, whatever the theory might be, a purely spiritual one.[1] A purely spiritual religion is necessarily an idealist religion, and so unreal. For the purely spiritual is the purely imaginary. It seemed, indeed, that modern Communism might well be that half of Christianity which had been dropped by the Church in favour of an accommodation with Rome, coming back to assert itself against the part that had been retained.

With this I was committed to rediscover a Christianity which is non-idealist. As a professional philosopher my part in this had to be largely theoretical; and in the remainder of this lecture I shall try to set out the main conclusions which I have reached so far. Among these was the growing sense that to be religious at all

[1] This may seem strange to students of medieval history. But I have no wish, even if it were possible, to deny either the wide claims of the medieval church to control every aspect of social life, nor her very real and practical services to the development of Western civilization and culture. The question, however, is not a historical but a religious one. Has this great organization of clerical power and privilege any valid claim to be the Church of Christ? The reform movements which led up to the Protestant Reformation implicitly denied this in their desire to return to what they believed to be the character of the apostolic Church. Above all, what was the medieval conception of the Christian life at its fullest and most religious? Was it not manifested in the religious orders, whose hall-mark was their withdrawal from the world? Such withdrawal *is* religious idealism.

27

is to be the member of a society, and I became increasingly unsatisfied in my isolation. So when I retired some years ago from university work, I looked to the Society of Friends, which alone was uninvolved in what stood between me and membership of the Churches, and which I could join without surrendering my freedom of conscience. I applied for admission, and I was graciously accepted. This membership of the Society of Friends has meant much to me, and I should like to take this opportunity to express my gratitude.

It is with this background of experience and judgment, and as a humble member of the Society of Friends that I offer for your consideration and judgment the conclusions which follow; about the meaning of religion, the nature of Christianity, the future form the Christian witness should take in the world and the place that Quakerism should covet in it.

SECOND MOVEMENT—
THE MEANING OF RELIGION

I HAVE tried to describe how, in my search for reality in religion, I was driven out of the organized Christian tradition; both on its theoretical side as theology and doctrine dogmatically affirmed and on its practical side, as a member of any Christian body. I was driven into a freedom which was lonely, painful and frightening. Loosed from the religious past, I remained in conviction religious, and in intention a Christian. Naturally, then, I was compelled to face the future and seek there what I could not find here and now. I had to ask what a wholly real religion might be and how it could be realized. I had to consider the future of religion. I had to enquire what was amiss with our Christianity and how it could be mended. In the remainder of this lecture I shall attempt to share with you the conclusions, necessarily personal and tentative, to which I have been led; and beyond this to say a little about the place that I see for our Quaker testimony in discovering and bringing into being this hope for the future.

What makes us human is our capacity for reflection. We not merely do things, but we know what we are doing. By reflecting on our behaviour we recognize success and failure. We devise rules for acting rightly and teach ourselves and our children to use them to direct and govern behaviour. So we develop an experience which we share with one another and which is passed on from generation to generation, increasing and deepening as it passes. Reflection, which makes this way of life possible, takes various forms. Science, art, philosophy, religion are all forms of reflection, through which, in various ways, we express and organize our growing experience and make it available for the future betterment of human life.

Now when we go back to the beginnings of human existence, we find only one form of reflection, and that form is religion. The others are contained in it; and in the course of social history they are gradually separated out, becoming independent and autonomous. But in the beginning there is only religion. It is then the sole form of reflection; and it is not only primary but also universal. Where there are men there is religion. How can we understand this?

Human life is always life in common. This does not mean merely that we live in groups. Animals also do this. But because of the place of reflection in human life, because we live by knowledge, the life of every one of us is a shared life. "What have you," said St. Paul, "that you have not received?" We are members of a community, in communication with one another. Primitive communities are relatively small. Their members are in direct relation with one another. They are enlarged families, with no separate, impersonal aspects of their lives, no political or economic activities which are not contained in the structure of personal relationship which unites them. And because their common life is an inclusive personal community, their reflective life is itself inclusive and personal. It is an expression of their consciousness of fellowship, which raises the fact of their common life to the level of intention. In reflection they are aware that they belong together in a personal unity; that all their activities are parts of the unity, and they rejoice in the awareness of it. This reflection is their religion. It sanctifies the common life and gives it meaning and purpose.

We can learn much about the nature of religion if we put ourselves, with sympathetic imagination, in the place of one of these ancient predecessors of ours and try to realize what his religion meant to him. It meant, in the first place, that he takes part, with the other members of his tribe in a common ceremonial activity, like a ritual dance, for example, or a ritual feast. But what is ritual? What is ceremonial? It is a common activity which is more than it seems, which carries a meaning beyond itself, which is symbolic. Our primitive ancestor is doing something with his fellows which is at once part of the common life and which expresses—which stands for or means—the commonness of their whole life. The dance or the feast means—We are all members of one another in the fellowship of daily life.

Another important feature of ritual is its persistence. Ritual activities have to be carried out strictly according to a traditional pattern which prescribes every detail. These come from the tribal past and are handed down with scrupulous care to posterity. The result is that participation in religious activity not merely expresses and so strengthens one's sense of belonging to the group of existing individuals who form the tribe today but also with the dead and with the yet unborn. So the tribe is felt as a unity of which its present members are merely the transient representatives. They come and go, but the tribe remains. They come from the tribe at birth and return to it at death. The ritual dance celebrates a personal relation with the dead as much as with the living. This is the first gift that primitive religion brings. It integrates the individual participants with one another and with their ancestors and their posterity in an undying personal unity. They are made conscious that they belong to the great family, and that they must maintain its way of life and transmit it unbroken to the future.

This is the central meaning, no doubt, of primitive religion, and, in a sense, I think, of all religion. We may formulate it, for reference, if we say that *Religion is about community*. But it has another aspect, which is already contained, by implication, in the first. The common life which religion brings to consciousness, which it expresses and confirms, is many-sided. It consists in varying sorts of co-operation which constitute the daily life of the tribe. It is both natural and inevitable that religious rituals should be specialized for reference to one or other of those forms of co-operation. The production and rearing of children is one. Co-operation in providing for the material needs of the tribe—of food especially—is another. These are the two fundamentals of the common life—work and marriage. You may recall the conclusion of the conference I described that we should never understand Christianity without a careful study of two things—communism and the sex problem. Now we find these two just as significant in primitive religion.

It is important to notice that modes of work as well as of marriage in primitive life are defined and ordered religiously. What we nowadays should consider secular and call "techniques" are themselves rituals of religion.

This is not easy for us to understand, so deeply established in us is the distinction between secular and sacred. We incline to distinguish the religious rituals which "accompany" primitive agriculture, for example, from the actual processes used in the cultivation of the soil. But primitive man could not draw such a distinction. His working life is all of a piece, and this wholeness is religious.

Nevertheless, primitive man is well aware that his working life is a co-operation with nature, and depends upon the forces of nature. So in the aspect we are considering, what his religion does for him is to unify him with the world in which he lives; and because this is conceived religiously it is conceived in personal terms; as a co-operation between him and a personal—not, mark you, a spiritual—world. The forces of nature are personal forces for him, and the religious activities which have reference to them are means of securing the good will of the world and for turning aside its wrath or malignity. So this aspect of primitive religion also is concerned with community—with the community between man and nature, of which the community between man and man is a part, though a part which has a unique significance, since we are men. In mature religion these two aspects have grown into the two great commandments, "Thou shalt love the Lord thy God" and "Thou shalt love thy neighbour as thyself". Of these two Jesus remarked that the second was similar to the first. Perhaps primitive religion can suggest to us in what this similarity consists.

I have directed your thoughts to primitive religion because it is easier to see in its very limitation and simplicity, the meaning and the structure of religion

33

at all its stages and in all its forms. I have selected, of course, those elements which I believe to be permanent through religious development. I have stressed the reference to community, and the two aspects which this must take—between man and the world and between man and man. I have left out any reference to the multifarious forms that primitive religious ritual takes. These are its means for achieving and maintaining the community it experiences. They are often grotesque and superstitious; they can be horrid and cruel and obscene. This is no doubt the reflection of their primitive childishness. For though it is truth of fact that God made Man in his own image, it is also true that man makes his conception of God in his, so that immature man has an immature conception of the Divine. These "primitive" characteristics gradually fade as human life develops, though not without relapses. But the underlying needs and experiences remain and with them the structure of religious meaning. I should like to add one thing more to the analysis, which might possibly explain why this religious structure takes the form it does. My conjecture is that it is governed by the sense of an unseen presence, of something more in our experience which is somehow personal, which transcends our familiar experience of life in common, and yet which faces us when we reflect deeply upon our everyday activities. In our own terms it is the experience of the presence of God.

One or two features of the process by which religion develops to maturity are important for our purpose. The first is that the usual process of social progress involves a struggle between progressive forces and the conservatism of religious authority. The result is the appearance of a distinction between the secular and the religious aspects of community life. Side by side with the religious leadership there arises a secular leadership, most often to begin with a leadership for war. The community loses its monolithic character and becomes dualist, with a tension between the two elements. The stage is set for the struggle between Church and State. There will be accommodations and concordats, of course; but the struggle for power between the two leaderships is inevitable and persistent. One form of accommodation is to distinguish between a spiritual and a material authority, and to limit the Church to the spiritual field and the State to the material. But in practice the two cannot be separated. They are interpenetrating and interdependent. Both Church and State must appeal to the same people for their loyalty and obedience. A spirituality that does not seek and secure its material embodiment is imaginary and unreal. A material life that is not spiritually directed is a meaningless quest of power and more power for its own sake. There may well be compromise, of course, but it will be inherently unstable, lasting only while neither is strong enough to subordinate the other to its own purposes. And in this process both religion and secular society must jeopardize their own integrity.

One society only, it would seem, achieved a progress to maturity without breaking the primitive bond of religious unity, and so escaped the surrender to dualism. This was the Hebrew society. It is precisely this fact that makes the Hebrews the uniquely religious people of history. That they are the religious people *par excellence* is clear. Why they are so is the important issue. So may I give you two pointers and leave you to follow them out. One might express it, in general, by saying that if a society *has* a religion, it is not religious. Conversely, a society such as the Hebrew people, which is fully religious, precisely because it *is* religious, does not *have* a religion. That is my first pointer. The second is like it. An earnest, intelligent Christian wrote a book to counter something I had written or said, and entitled it, "Was Jesus a social reformer?" His answer to this question was, in effect, that Jesus was not a social reformer but a religious teacher. To this one can only reply by asking "How could Jesus or any Hebrew prophet, or any Hebrew at all, for that matter, be a religious teacher without being a social reformer, or a social reformer without being a religious teacher?" The distinction between religion and politics does not exist in a theocratic[1] society.

So much for the distinction between the religious and the secular aspects of society. The second important difference between primitive and mature religion which we must notice is this. Primitive religion is always the religion of an actual and limited group. Its god is the god of the tribe or nation and every tribe or nation has its own particular god. A mature religion, on the contrary, is universal. It is for all mankind, and its god is the only true God. In other words, it is monotheistic. Monotheism clearly implies universality. If there is only one true God then the gods of the nations are not real gods at all. Equally the peoples

[1] The term "theocratic" has no place in the theory of politics. In applying it to the Hebrew society of the Old Testament I mean only that the law which regulates all aspects of its life is religious. Its sanction is that it is the revealed will of God.

of the world must owe allegiance to the one God. But apart from this, religion is, in its very nature, implicitly universal. Primitive religion fails to realize this because the basis of the tribal unity which it serves is a blood-relationship. The tribe is a kinship group. There is a natural confusion, in reflecting on the unity of the tribe, between common descent from the same ancestors, with the unity of personal relationship. In fact, the brotherhood which religion expresses and seeks to achieve is personal, not organic. It rests upon affection. It may be natural for blood-relations to love one another, but it is by no means inevitable; and any group of persons who are united by mutual affection form a personal fellowship even if they have no blood relationship. This can be expressed most simply by noting that any two people in the world can be friends. Friendship is a spiritual relationship, and in this sense any religious unity is a spiritual, not a biological unity. In quite primitive groups this is evidenced, if not understood, by the ubiquitous ceremonies of "blood-brotherhood", in which a stranger is brought into the tribal community through a ritual pretence of blood-relationship. As soon as the development of society unites people of different tribal origins, the non-organic basis is forced into consciousness and the universal religions are on the horizon.

Now a universal religion, as any full-grown religion must be, is in a quandary. Any religion involves a united brotherhood whose religion it is. But a universal religion must require a universal brotherhood. With the realization of the inherent universality of religion, the tribe or nation becomes mankind. But, in fact, there is no such universal fellowship. Mankind is split

37

up into a heterogeneous collection of peoples, nations, tribes which are not in fellowship, and which are in rivalry or even in enmity or in "a state of war, with their weapons pointing at one another's vitals", as Hobbes put it. This is the fundamental problem for all the great religions. *Whose* religion are they, and what is the bond of personal union which they celebrate and sanctify?

There are several ways in which the solution may be sought. But before we look at them, we should notice that the fact that generates the recognized universality of religion is a fact about the character of human society. It is the fact that it is not a biological unity, not based on blood-relation, but a personal unity; and in the sense I have just noted, a spiritual unity. Even the natural family is united as a human group, if and because its members love one another. If they do not, their kinship will not prevent the family from disintegrating. But this fact implies also that there is an inherent impulse in human nature to break through its organic limitations and realize itself as a great society to which all men belong. If the corollary of any religion is a community then the corollary of a universal religion is a universal community. With the appearance of the universal religions, the disunity of mankind becomes a failure, a tragedy, an evil to be deplored and a sin to be confessed. Mankind *ought to be* a single community.

One way to deal with the problem is to set out to unify the world by force. Many of the existing human societies have in fact been created in this way—by unification through conquest. In a few generations they accept their unity as a natural phenomenon, and become conscious of it and loyal to it. This solution is associated in particular with Islam, at least in its earlier days. There are two reasons why this solution is a false one. Even if the conquest were successful, it could not produce a *religious* unity. The means would destroy the end. You cannot make people love one another by force. A successful conquest of the world would involve a rejection of the religion it was supposed to realize. The second reason is that it could not be successful. Force calls out a counter force, and the counter force in the end, must be stronger. Two world wars in one century have proved it to us; but the old story of the Roman Empire is even more convincing. Everyone, including the leaders of Islam, recognizes today the absurdity and the folly of using force to secure religious ends.

A second way to deal with the problem of universality is the idealist way, which is seen in its simplest and most unadulterated form in Buddhism. It consists in denying the reality of the everyday world, in which the conflict and disunity appear. The world of the senses is the world of illusion. The ideal is the real. It would follow from this that the disunity, the struggle, the suffering of this material world is illusory. We have only to turn our eyes away from it, overcome the desires which bind us to its unreality, and learn to live in the real world, where all is unity and peace.

Idealism takes many forms, and the forms that concern us more nearly we shall have to consider later. For the moment we need only notice that at the core of such solutions lies a withdrawal from the world, and this means that the problem is solved by denying it. The universal community to which religion refers is

39

not of this world but of another: a world to which we can find entrance by discovering our own reality—our spiritual reality—and by withdrawing our interest from the foolish purposes for which in this world men labour and struggle. This, in turn, is no solution. One does not solve a problem by persuading oneself that there is really no problem to be solved, or by transferring it to a world of ideas where all that is needed for the solution is to think differently. The problem is a practical one—a problem in *action*. It cannot be solved by thinking. Idealism, in general, seeks to attach our emotions to ideas. This is what is meant by saying that the Real is the Idea. Whatever may be thought of this as philosophy—and in my judgment it is bad philosophy—it meets no real need and solves no practical issue. Ideas refer to things not things to ideas. They are true or false according to the rightness or wrongness of their reference to the world of things. In themselves they are nothing: they are imaginary. Their function is to guide our action in the real world—in the world of things which is the only world in which we can act. Certainly idealism is incompatible with Christianity, if only because it makes nonsense of the life and death of Christ.

If then we put these unreal solutions aside, we can turn to our proper question. "What is the Christian solution to the problem of the universality of religion?" This is really the central question about the inherent character of Christianity itself, about the *meaning* of Christianity.

THIRD MOVEMENT—
THE MEANING OF CHRISTIANITY

To understand Christianity it is completely necessary to begin with the Old Testament; that is to say, with the documents from which we can reconstruct the story of the development of Hebrew religion. Jesus himself presupposed and indeed asserted the religious validity of the Law and the Prophets. He conceived his own mission to be its fulfilment. But for our present purpose it will be sufficient to contrast the Jewish answer to the problem of religious universality with the two which we have already discussed and which we have found exemplified in Islam and in Buddhism respectively.

Hebrew religion is unique, I have suggested, in its capacity to retain the all-inclusive character of primitive religion through the long process of its development to maturity. At the centre of this development lies the struggle against dualism. It is clear from the records that Hebrew religion began as a tribal religion, worshipping the God of Abraham and Isaac and Jacob, the religion of the children of Israel. Its earliest stage of growth is a struggle against "idolatry"; a struggle to exclude the worship of other gods than their own, which is summed up in the "first commandment—Thou shalt have no other gods before Me". This struggle laid the foundation of the fierce monolatry of their early social life; a monolatry which in distinguishing clearly their own God from the gods of the nations round about, established the general social exclusiveness which has marked Jewish life ever since. On the basis of this exclusive devotion to their own God, and the exclusiveness of their social life which made them a peculiar people, contrasted and contrasting themselves with the heathen round about, the teaching of their prophets led them from monolatry to a full and uncompromising monotheism, through the denial that the gods of the heathen are real gods; and the corresponding assertion that their God is the only true God.

The struggle against dualism is the struggle to keep religion the fundamental ordering force that directs and unifies all the aspects of social life. Any dualism of classes—master class and slave class, aristocrats and plebeians, rulers and workers—makes such a religious unity impossible, since it breaks the bond of brotherhood. Two of the ways in which such dualisms may arise in the development of a society from its primitive religious unity are the perpetuation of debt-slavery so that the poor become permanently subservient to the rich; and the rise to domination of a priestly caste through their monopoly of culture and law. Both these processes threatened the Hebrew community and both were provided against. The first was negatived by the institution of the year of Jubilee; the second by the distinction between priest and prophet. Priests and Levites form a distinct group; they could well become a dominant class but for one thing. The word of the Lord comes to the prophet, and the prophet may be anyone. He may be a priest or he may be a herdsman; but whoever he is, it is he who is the direct and living messenger of God. The priesthood that would become a dominant ruling class must combine both functions;

42

it must be at once the servant of the cult and the intermediary between God and the people.

In Hebrew history the main danger of dualism was associated with the setting up of the kingship. The account given in the Old Testament is curiously ambivalent. The demand for a king comes from the people, and their reason is said to be the desire to be like the nations round about. The demand is said to be a rebellion against God; yet it is by the command of God that the popular desire is satisfied; and the king is chosen by God.

It may well be that something of this kind was becoming necessary. The danger was that the king should become the centre of a secular authority which would limit the sphere of religion; and so change radically the *meaning* of the Hebrew people. And this danger is expressed, in fact, in the desire to be "like the nations round about". To prevent this it was necessary that the kingship should itself be given a place within the religious structure, that it should have a religious function in the community. This is what makes the reign of David so significant, as a man after God's own heart; and even more significant is the manner in which he remained, in Jewish memory, *the* king *par excellence*. The history of the kingship shows how real the danger was; and in the end it was the religious conception of the people which triumphed, possibly because only through it could their survival as a distinct people be achieved, as it has been achieved through the centuries to our own time; although they have been scattered among the nations with nothing but their religion to hold them together.

To this we should add that the Gospels make much

43

of the claim of Jesus, as son of David, to be the King of the Jews; and this was the title under which, by the cruel irony of the Roman governor, he was crucified. But in accepting the title he transformed it into a wholly religious leadership, by the rejection of secular power. "My kingdom is not of this world," he said; "If it were then would my servants fight."

Now, so soon as monotheism is established, religion is universalized. If there is only one God, then he is the God of the whole earth, the God and Father of all men. How then can he remain the God of this exclusive and peculiar people, the Jews? How did the Hebrews deal with this problem, which clearly could not be escaped? I must reduce the full answer to its barest outlines for reasons of space; though, in fact, it includes in its scope the whole character and meaning of the mature religious reflection of the Hebrew people.

To begin with, then, the one God is the Creator of heaven and earth and all that is in them, of all life and of man whom He made in his own image. In our terminology God is the original, unlimited and universal agent. The Hebrew prophet, in contrast to the Greek philosopher, conceives reality as the product and field of activity of a free, creative agent; and he conceives human reality in the same terms. Man, made in the image of God, is also a free and creative agent, within the limits prescribed by the intention of his Creator. Many things follow from this: first, since all men are the children of Adam, they are in the nature of things, one family. But as a matter of fact, they are not. Not only are they different peoples, but they are rivals, and at enmity, or even at war with one another. At once we face the problem of evil—not

44

the problem of ignorance, as in the thought of Socrates or Plato. God made the world and saw that it was good. But it isn't. How can this be? It can be because man, made in the image of God, has the freedom to create and seek to realize his own intentions. These intentions may be incompatible with the divine intention in his creation. Evil then is sin and sin is a personal conflict of wills. Since religion is about community, a clash of wills between men and God must express itself in the breaking of community—as a clash of wills between man and man. Indeed since the purpose of God for man *is* man's true nature, in being at enmity with God he is at odds with himself.

This is the first part of the answer to the problem of evil. But as it stands it is incomplete. It would mean that God's creation is a failure. But this is impossible. There can be nothing in the world which is capable of thwarting the purpose of the Creator.[1] The will of God *must* prevail. This means that though man can set his will against God's—since God has made him so—he cannot do it successfully. In the end he must capitulate to "that of God in him", which is his inmost nature, his own reality demanding its realization. The purpose

---

[1] Demythologizers and searchers for a "modern image" of God may take exception to the language of these paragraphs. While welcoming the claim for freedom of thought in religion which they embody, I believe that there is a danger that they should go too far. Science cannot provide canons for religious language. Probably all religious language, certainly all religious language about God, must contain a mythological element, since it must speak, in terms of our ordinary experience, of what lies beyond it. The highest, richest and rarest qualities in our experience of human personality, such as creative spontaneity, provide the most adequate basis for our characterization of God. Even these, of course, are inadequate, and we have to use them mythologically. God is beyond the personal, of course; but it is the personal in our experience which points in the direction of God, and provides the most adequate language we possess for references to God.

of God is the establishing of a permanent co-operative fellowship between Man and Himself, which must be achieved with full human consent; and the corollary of this is the restoration of a universal community of mankind by doing away with the enmity between man and man.

The second part of the answer then is that the divine creation is continuing. It goes on. God did not become a sleeping partner with the creation of Man. If Man has set his will against God's (as clearly he has) the purpose of God still stands and must be realized. In the recognition of the Fall there is already the promise of a redemption. And to see this is to discover history, as the Hebrews did, and with it a religious interpretation of history as the work of God for the salvation of the world, in spite of and even through the opposition of human wills.

We can now see the Hebrew answer to the problem of a universal religion. The one true God, the God of the whole earth remains the God of the Hebrew people in a unique sense. This is possible because the Hebrews discover themselves as the chosen people. How chosen? Chosen by God as his instrument for the redemption of the world, and the achievement of his purpose of finally setting up His kingdom upon earth, and reuniting the broken fragments of mankind in a single fellowship of peace. This is the meaning of the covenant with Abraham, when God said, "In thee and in thy seed shall all the nations of the earth be blessed."

Here then, we have discovered a third solution to the problem of religious universality. It is a practical and a historical solution. The community which corresponds to the universal religion, can be both the brotherhood of mankind and the particular human society which is unified by the worship of the one true God. The two communities are related as end and means. The second is the instrument for the realization of the first. It is, as it were, a prototype of the first, since it is the community which is actually unified and directed by the religion which will in due course unify and direct the community of mankind. Its intention and its meaning lies not in itself but beyond itself. It exists, not for itself, but for the world.

This great religious insight was brought to consciousness in the history of the Hebrews only fitfully, in flashes of prophetic insight. Its implications were slowly and gradually revealed. But it led to an increasing spirituality and inwardness, and to a growing understanding of what constitutes a truly human fellowship and how alone it can be created and sustained. To the other religious insights of the Hebrew people it added a sense of destiny, the expectation of a consummation in the future. And at the centre of the hope lay the promise of a coming Messiah who would establish the Kingdom of Heaven on the earth.

* * * * *

In the fullness of time the Messiah came, in the person of Jesus of Nazareth, the son of Joseph the carpenter. About the age of thirty He came to Jordan to be baptized by John. There is no need for me to retell the short story of His public ministry, the most tragic and the most decisive story in the history of mankind. He came to His own, calling them to repentance, proclaiming the advent of the kingdom, offering Himself as their leader. The rulers were against Him from the first, though at first the common people were attracted. But when His meaning became clear and the implications of repentance appeared, they soon left Him, all but a handful of bewildered disciples. He went about, teaching and doing good, and in three years He was decisively rejected by His own people, condemned by their rulers as a blasphemer who deserved death; and on their instigation judged and sentenced to death and crucified by order of the Roman governor. Religious and secular authority joined hands successfully to defeat and destroy Him by the way of the cross; and by the way of the cross He won the decisive victory in the battle for the world's redemption.

The meaning of that life and death is infinite and inexhaustible. Here I want to draw your attention to the aspect of it which carries further our study of religion as the consciousness of community. From the beginning of His ministry Jesus considered Himself to have a mission, to have been sent by God, whom He called His Father, to the Jewish people to announce the coming of the Kingdom of Heaven. This suggests, if it does not actually imply, that He thought of Himself as the Messiah, and I find it difficult to make anything of the story of the temptation in the wilderness, however it is to be interpreted, unless He is thinking of Himself in this way. It is characteristic of the Hebrew prophets that their message is a call to repentance; and it arises through interpreting the present situation and condition of the people in the light of their past, and of the obligations it imposes. Now the situation in which Jesus finds His people is new. They are part of the

Roman Empire under Augustus, which has imposed the Roman peace throughout the Mediterranean world, after generations of continuous warfare and strife. There is a famous poem of Virgil's in which he celebrates this achievement, and which is referred to from an early period as the "Messianic Eclogue". For the early church interpreted it as a prophecy in praise of Christ, the Prince of Peace. Within the Empire, the Jews, like other peoples, enjoyed a large measure of self-government and the right to practise their own religion, subject only to recognizing the sovereignty of Caesar and paying tribute to him. To Jesus, meditating in the wilderness upon the mission He must undertake, the question of the relation of the Jewish people to the Roman Empire must have arisen and demanded a decision. Are they to accept the Roman Empire or to reject it? The answer which is embodied in His public life and teaching would seem to be this: God working out His will in history has set up the Roman Empire, and set the Jewish people in it. To this extent we must accept it as the will of God. On the other hand, the Roman Empire, though it has established peace and united the nations, cannot be the promised Kingdom; though it must be a necessary stage in the way towards it. The reason is that it is not a true community. It has been created by military conquest and it is maintained by self-interest and in the last analysis, by compulsion. Its basis, therefore, is fear. But the Kingdom of Heaven cannot be created by force. It must be freely chosen. It cannot be maintained by self-interest but only by self-sacrifice, and in the end, by attraction. For its basis cannot be fear; it can only be love.

What then is the task set by these conditions for the Jewish people, who are the people chosen by God as the instrument for His purpose, the realization of the universal human community, which is the salvation of the world? It cannot be to reject the Empire, if this means to take up arms in a heroic struggle for freedom and independence. Not because such a struggle must be unsuccessful. That might not matter. But because it would be, in spiritual fact, the acceptance of the Roman way of compulsion and conquest. A Jewish Empire would be no more the Kingdom of Heaven than a Roman one. The only possible alternative is to remain within the Empire while rejecting its spiritual basis, and to transform it from within into a true community. The way to do this was plain. The people must repent and return to their full allegiance to God; and so become what they were meant to be—a true human fellowship as revealed in the scriptures. In this way, defenceless but without fear, they should exhibit in the Empire, to the Empire, the image of the fellowship of mankind as God intends it and as man, if it were not for his fear, must desire it. They must rely upon love and attraction instead of fear and compulsion, and meet the strength of Rome in the power of the spirit of God.

Such, in outline, is the account I am constrained to give, after long consideration, of the task to which Jesus called His own people when He took up His mission. It has two main sources. The first is the implications of His acceptance of the office of Messiah, coupled with His rejection of the line of thought which would have made Him a military leader. The other is His own teaching as it is recorded in the Gospels, particularly in the parables of the Kingdom. This is not the place to defend my interpretation, if it needs defence. It provides an inclusive framework within which all that is essential can find its place. What it excludes is only that type of interpretation which would cut the work of Jesus loose from its place in history and its reference to history, and present it as though it were timeless and general. He was a Hebrew prophet, not a Greek philosopher, and therefore He was concerned with the fulfilment of God's purpose in history to redeem His creation. He came for the salvation of the world, and taught His disciples to pray, "Thy Kingdom come, Thy will be done on earth."

But the call to His own people to fulfil their destiny under His leadership was rejected, and Jesus recognized that His mission would end in defeat and death. At that point He began to concentrate His attention upon the small band of His faithful disciples to prepare them for carrying on His task when He should be gone. They were the remnant who had accepted Him; and since the Jews of His time were themselves only the remnant of the original twelve tribes of Israel, they were only the remnant of a remnant. Yet upon them fell the task of carrying out the purpose which should have fallen upon the Hebrew people as a whole. This small group of believing Jews became, of course, the Christian Church in the world. It is important, therefore, to note and to remember always, that the function to which it is called is not a new one. The purpose of God has not changed, nor the necessity of a human co-operation in its fulfilment. The Church's task is the task to which the whole people of Israel were called and for which they were chosen. What has changed is the situation of His disciples after the death of Jesus. They are no longer looking for the coming of the Messiah. He has come and has been rejected and crucified. He has gone and they are alone. The Gospel they have to proclaim is the same good news of the coming on earth of the Kingdom of Heaven but it now contains the news of His coming, of His life and death for the redemption of the world, and of the revelation of the nature of God and the purpose of God that He embodied. In fact, because of His life and death the Kingdom of Heaven has already come. They themselves are not merely the witnesses to the gospel, but the first citizens of the kingdom. All this and much more is added; but it is not substituted for what went before. There is a new understanding, a new conviction, and a new guarantee that the redemption will be fully achieved. But the task itself is unchanged.

I have omitted any reference to the Resurrection of Jesus, in order to keep strictly to the historical field. That His tomb was found empty is an historical statement, for which the evidence is strong. That Jesus appeared after His death to His disciples on several occasions is a statement of a different order. That they were wholly and sincerely convinced by these appearances that He had "risen from the dead" and was alive again, is completely certain. Their subsequent behaviour and their power to convince so many others would be inexplicable if it were not so. Yet these appearances were also disappearances. No one imagines that Jesus was then living in hiding and paying occasional visits to His followers. The appearances have the character of visions, and it is noteworthy that Paul reckoned his vision of Jesus on the road to Damascus as one of them. (See 1 Cor. 15, v. 8.) So this "life from the dead" must be life of a new kind, of which life as we know it, can be only an indication and which can only be characterized in mythological terms. If, then, we speak in historical terms, His disciples are truly alone, and in their aloneness they expect that He will "come again".

What meaning, then, can we give to the resurrection? If it is to have a religious meaning for us now, it must be for us now a religious experience. Mere assent to an ancient historical claim, however well attested, can of itself have no religious meaning. All religion, I believe, rests on the experience of the presence of God. This experience manifests itself in feelings of awe and self-abasement, but it does not reveal the nature of God, only His majesty and power. This is why there is such variety in the conception of God in different religions. For the Christian, in his worship of God, there is, however, another experience, that of the presence of Jesus Christ in and amongst the worshippers. And this presence seems, as it were, to coalesce with, or join itself to the presence of God, in such fashion as to provide the image of God that we need. This is *our* experience of His resurrection, and with it of His relation to God. For we can express this experience only by saying, "He is not dead, He is risen." Christ Jesus lives in us and in the world, manifesting the nature of the God we worship and working through us to create the fulness of the Kingdom of God on earth.

I do not propose to attempt any exposition of the teaching of Jesus. It speaks for itself to those who have ears to hear. The one rule which I have found essential in seeking to understand it is an obvious one, though it is often disregarded. It is this. We must take it for granted that He means just what He says; and that He knows better than any commentator how to say what He means. Beyond this there are a few suggestions that may prove helpful to others as they have to me. His teaching is intensely practical and very realistic. He deals with facts and looks towards action. He avoids general rules and instead seeks to convey and to illustrate an attitude of mind. He is no philosopher, least of all a theologian or moralist. He does not write books. He speaks to people; sometimes to a solitary individual, sometimes to His disciples, sometimes to the multitude; but whoever His hearers may be He speaks to their condition. I sometimes think that if we could ask Him the moralist's question, "Why can I not do as I please?" He might well answer, "Well! Why can't you? Let's find out and put it right!" Above all, His teaching looks always to the task to be accomplished and the means for its accomplishing. He is concerned, that is to say, to make clear, to His disciples in particular, the character of the Christian community which He will leave behind Him to carry on His work, and the conditions which it must fulfil if it is to do so. When He says, for example, "Love your enemies", this is the statement of a necessary condition for replacing enmity by affection and so achieving reconciliation. It is a pragmatic rule for the work of the Church in extending the Kingdom of Heaven in the world.

It is a long time since Pentecost, and the history of the Christian Church has been one of success and failure, of back-sliding and return. Some of its aberrations have been shocking in the extreme to any

Christian judgment. After nearly two thousand years we find ourselves broken into pieces, yet spread throughout the length and breadth of the earth. The internal struggles between our sections are moderating and we are moving—hesitatingly and unsurely—towards a reunion. Yet at a time when the Church is beginning to deserve more trust and more attention than for many centuries, those parts of the world which had submitted to its claims are moving towards disbelief and disregard. We have to face a future in which we shall be increasingly rejected, at a time when the Christian message is more patently necessary and more clearly relevant than it has ever been. Our need is to rediscover, under contemporary conditions, what sort of community we ought to be in the world, and to become that kind of community. It is to rediscover and to fulfil the conditions which are requisite for accomplishing the task committed to us.

With these things in mind, I feel constrained to indicate what seem to me to be the major failures of the Church to be what it was designed to be, and to perform the function for which it was established. I shall not concern myself with details, but only with the general, persistent and deep-seated mistakes and misjudgments.

First in time and in persistence I should put the infection of dualism. Already by the second century A.D. there are clear evidences of the influence of Greek thought upon the understanding of the Christian mission. This is by no means easy to express, because it concerns the form rather than the substance of the matter. When an early Greek, who has sought for a satisfying view of the world and of human life in one

55

philosophical school after another, finally discovers Christianity and says, "Now I have found the true philosophy", he is conceiving Christianity on a Greek analogy. He is, no doubt unconsciously, treating the Hebrew prophet as if he were a Greek philosopher. The difference, if for a moment I may use a technical term, is a difference of *apperception*; a difference not so much in what is thought as in the way of thinking. So when a Greek philosopher, like Plato, is convinced that for a human being death is not the end of everything, he formulates a doctrine of the immortality of the soul. In the same situation the Hebrew prophet would enunciate his belief in the resurrection of the body.

It is the effect of this dualism upon Christianity that concerns us. It shifts the emphasis from action to thought, from practice to theory. Greek thought is fundamentally dualist. It distinguishes clearly between work and reflection, and makes reflection primary. Both Plato and Aristotle agree that the good life is the life of contemplation. So they do not think of God as the Creator, but as engaged in eternal contemplation. Man, likewise, is a thinker, not a worker. Labour is for lesser men, incapable of realizing the full possibilities of human existence. Dualist thought is in terms of contraries which are brought into opposition, and between which a choice has to be made. Matter and mind is one pair; others are body and spirit, spiritual life and material life; the spiritual world and the material world. But the fundamental contrast is between the theoretical and the practical.

The general influence of Greek philosophy upon Christianity has been profound. Augustine was a Neoplatonist before he became a Christian—though the Neoplatonist influence within the Church had begun earlier. Thomas Aquinas preferred to use the Aristotelian philosophy. Stoicism also affected Christian thought, particularly in the field of morality; so much so indeed that when modern people refer to Christian morality, it is usually Stoic morality which they are talking about without knowing it.

What then has been, in general terms, the effect of this long impact upon Christianity of Greek modes of thought? The first is that it transferred the emphasis, within Christianity, from practice to theory. Faith, which originally meant trust and confidence, came to mean a set of beliefs. Christians came to be people who professed certain beliefs. Christianity, aiming at the philosophic ideal, sought to become an organized system of doctrine. This assimilation of Christianity to Greek philosophy not only created theology. It created heresy. Instead of saying, with Jesus, "By their fruits ye shall know them", we found ourselves thinking that Christians are to be known by their opinions. Intellectual activity, when it is used by itself as a standard of truth, is necessarily divisive. It created all the competing philosophic schools of Greece; and equally in the Church it created competing systems of doctrine. Then, to prevent the disintegration of the Church, one system had to be established as the proper system, by the fiat of the rulers of the Church. Heretics became enemies of the faith, to be suppressed or exterminated. The time came, however, when the Church lost the power to enforce unity of belief by spiritual threats or physical violence, and the Christian Church began to divide into the sects that we know today, and of which we Friends are one.

One other effect from which we suffer today should perhaps be mentioned. If a belief becomes an accepted part of a system which defines a religion, then whoever denies it, however good his reasons, is proclaiming his disloyalty to the community. If, for example, the Church guarantees that the earth is the centre of the heavenly bodies, it is impossible, without disloyalty, to give proofs that the sun is the centre of a solar system in which this earth is a planet. This is the main reason for the conflict between Christianity and science, or indeed between science and religion in general. It is highly dangerous to include, in a statement of religious belief, anything that is liable to empirical disproof.

The second effect I must mention is the emergence of idealism in Christianity. It is at least probable that a religion which accepts dualism is logically committed to idealism. In any case it was the idealist tradition in Greek philosophy, which was created by Plato, and particularly in its Neoplatonist form, which affected Christianity most profoundly. The essential thing about dualism, as we have seen, is that it contrasts the material with the spiritual in such a way as to bring them into opposition. This opposition forces us to choose between them, and the idealist choice is for the reality, and so the importance, of the spiritual. An idealist religion, then, is concerned with the spiritual life, and *not* with the material, and the life of the spirit can be achieved only at the expense of the material life. This is the root of the tendency to treat the body and its desires as in themselves sinful and the source of evil. It is also the source, at the other extreme, of the view that the highest form of religious experience is mystical.

It is easy to see that a religion infected with such an attitude must be in some sense "otherworldly". It is not, that is to say, primarily concerned with this world, but with the cultivation of the spiritual life. This means, again, a withdrawal from the world—into a monastery, for example. Here another aspect of idealism reveals itself. It is naturally egocentric or self-interested. To withdraw from the world is to withdraw into oneself. The spiritual life, if it is opposed to the material, is solitary. It consists in ideas and emotions, in thoughts and imaginings and words. These however, have no meaning and no reality in themselves, but only through their reference to things and beings which exist in their own right, not merely in our minds. Religious idealism in face of the obvious need for such a reference, provides it in *another* world, a spiritual world with which we can have occasional communion, in prayer and meditation, when we withdraw from *this* world; in a better world which that which is immortal in us will inherit when death has finally freed us from the burden of our material bodies.

All this—and I feel sure you will recognize it—is excellent Platonism. But it is not Christian at all. I have grave doubts, indeed, whether idealism, in any form, is compatible with religion. Religion is concerned in its reality with two things—with action and with community. Idealism seeks to escape from action into meditation; and from the tensions of life in common into the solitariness of one's own spirit. The purely spiritual which it seeks is the purely imaginary, a ghost world without substance or shadow. Jesus came to proclaim, not a way of escape from the world, but the coming of the Kingdom of Heaven within it.

Christianity is concerned with an earthly world that needs redemption; not with a heavenly other-world which is eternally perfect.

This absorption of Greek idealism paved the way for the third, and, in my view, the decisive effect. This was the acceptance, by the Church, of the Roman Empire. The history books refer to it as the acceptance of Christianity by Rome; but of course Rome never accepted Christianity, except, one might possibly say, in an emasculated form which offered no challenge to her secular authority. Indeed, it became the business of the Church to provide, in general principle, a divine sanction for the society maintained by Roman power and prestige. This, indeed, is the function of any established church. And it rests upon the acceptance of dualism by both Church and State. Thereafter there are two swords—the temporal sword wielded by the State and the spiritual sword which is wielded by the Church. Notice that both Emperor and Pope carry swords. The symbolism means that Christianity has become a kind of spiritual politics. The struggle for power has been established within the Church as it has always been within the State. There are not merely two systems of law, but two systems of morality: one for the men of religion, who have withdrawn from the world and its secular interests, the other for those who remain in a worldly calling.

The influence of the Roman Empire upon the Church which had accepted it, was as profound as the influence of Greek philosophy. It is, in a sense, more practical, concerned more with the technical aspects of life—with organization, administration and government. It introduced into the history of Christianity the second of the major divisive elements, the competition between different systems of church government. The very phrase indicates how politically-minded the Church has become. But this is too large a subject to pursue now. It must suffice to mention it. The essential point to notice is this. In accepting the invitation to become the religion of the Roman Empire, Christianity had to refer its teaching, even where it has clear social implications, to another world. Now it wields a sword; but it is a spiritual sword only, not a temporal one. Its task is not to transform the Roman State into the Kingdom of Heaven, but to sanctify the secular order. The rewards and punishments which sanction its authority are in the next world. This world is transitory and in itself unimportant. What importance it has lies in the fact that how we live here will determine our fate in the world after death. In a word, with the acceptance of this dualistic organization of society the Christian teachings must be referred away from this world to another. They no longer refer to the world in which we live. This, let me remind you, is the burden of the Marxist attack on religion, and it is, in general, justified. For if the people of the world were to say to the Church, "We are convinced; we wish to live in the Kingdom of Heaven that you have taught us about. Will you set it up for us?"[1] the Church would have to say (would it not?), "Oh, no! That is a material question! That is not our business! If you want a new kind of society to live in you must go to the State." And they *are* turning to the State, away from the Church, in increasing numbers with

[1] This is, of course, the wrong question to ask; but in a dualist society like ours, it is a natural one.

every generation. This too, by and large, is justified; though it cannot be successful.

These aberrations of the Christian Church, which are of such long standing that they are now, for most people, identified with Christianity, are with us still. It is time to turn to the contemporary Church, therefore, and in the light of this study of the past, to consider its future.

FINALE—
THE FUTURE OF THE CHURCH

IN this final section of my lecture, when I turn to consider not the past, but the present and future, I wish to speak as a Friend to Friends. I have been a member of your fellowship for too short a time to understand fully and naturally all the implications of your tradition: so I ask for your forbearance. I have to set out what I believe to be the changes that are demanded of the Christian Church today, in view of the future which we face. I shall do so as clearly as I can, and without qualifications. I trust that you will believe that I am submitting myself, with diffidence and in Christian humility, to your judgment, desiring as much to be instructed as to instruct.

May I begin with a personal statement that may make for understanding. There have been Christian writers and preachers in recent times who have insisted that Christianity is not a religion. I confess that I have found it difficult to discover what precisely is meant by such a contrast between religion and Christianity. But if there were such a contrast, and if I were driven to choose between them, I should have no hesitation. I should choose Christianity and let religion go. I have always considered myself a Christian, though I have had and still have difficulty in discovering how effectively to be a Christian; and by this I mean that I have desired and do desire to discover what it means to be a disciple of Jesus, in order to be one. I take it for granted, I think rightly, that the Society of Friends is also Christian, and I often wish that we might feel constrained to proclaim ourselves not merely a religious but also a Christian Society of Friends.

There is, perhaps, one way in which the contrast between Christianity and religion might be drawn, though I think incorrectly. There is a widespread conception of religion as the cultivation of a refined spirituality. In one form it makes mysticism central; so that religion would seem to stem from mystical experience and to culminate in it. But in commoner forms it is the view that religion is for the benefit of the worshipper; reassuring, comforting and strengthening him, and securing for him the grace and favour of God. To make the essential point as simply as possible, it is a way of talking or thinking that assumes that religion is for the sake of the worshipping community, in one sense or another.

Now if religion is this, then it stands in strong contrast with Christianity as I understand it. Christianity is not for the sake of the Christians but *for the sake of the world*. The Christian Church exists not for the spiritual benefit of its members but for the salvation of the world outside it. This is the task assigned to it by Jesus, and it is the continuance of His work after His death. In the light of this we may venture a functional definition of the Church. "The Church", we may say, "is the community of the disciples of Jesus working, in co-operation with God and under the guidance of His Spirit, to establish the Kingdom of Heaven on earth."

I do not, however, believe that this contrast of religion and Christianity is valid. It arises from the dualism of spiritual and material; and this, in turn, from isolating the spiritual from its material reference.

The basic dualism is between thought and action. Now there can be thought without action, but no action without thought. The material life is the spirit in practical expression, and so in *reality*. Consequently what a man believes is expressed in his way of life. If what he professes to believe differs from this, then either he is mistaken about what he believes or he is hypocritical. The spiritual life is this without the action, which alone could make it real. It is then the spirit functioning in imagination, and it can be real only through its reference to action: apart from this it is wholly imaginary.

Religion is about action because it is concerned with the whole man. A religion which is concerned only with the "spiritual life" is a religion which leaves action out, and in which spiritual activity has no practical reference. To define Christianity as we have just done—in practical terms—is not to *exclude* the spiritual but precisely to *include* it together with the practical reference that gives it its meaning and its reality. The point I am stressing is that for the Christian, the meaning and purpose of his religion lies outside himself and not within him. He is a person "for others", as Jesus was; a person dedicated to the salvation of the world. This also means, however, that he is a member of a Christian community in the world, which is itself dedicated to the salvation of the world, and which can only achieve this by exhibiting, in its own action in the world, the image of the Kingdom of Heaven.

I have stressed this issue at length because I believe it to be fundamental for us at the present point in history. With our brethren of all nations and races we are passing through the widest and deepest of social

revolutions. We live in a day of judgment. The whole
earth is being shaken down to the deepest roots of
human life; and these are religious. Whatever cannot
stand in the judgment will be destroyed. One does not
need to be a prophet to realize that mankind stands
before a choice between self-destruction and some form
of effective world-unity. If this unity is established, the
situation which Jesus faced in the Roman Empire
will be re-established, but this time on a world scale;
and the Christian Church will be faced with the task
of its transformation from a worldly unity of organization and administration backed by overwhelming
force into the brotherhood of the Kingdom of Heaven.

In this situation the Christian Church, in especial,
falls under judgment. What will be swept away, what
will remain, and what will be changed we do not yet
know, and perhaps we should not try to guess. But
we can believe that there must be a transformation,
which will affect every branch and section of the Church
and not least our own Society of Friends. For the
Church, in all its sections, and in all its modes of
activity, material and spiritual alike, is clearly inadequate—or so it seems to me—to the task that lies
ahead of us. There must be a reformation and a new
beginning. For this, it may seem to you, as it does to
me, that the question we have been discussing is
central. It is the rediscovery of the religious reference.
Religion, like all reflective activities, is symbolic.
Religious activities, in the narrow sense, have a
meaning beyond themselves. Only through their
reference to the world of ordinary, non-reflective
experience, have they any point or any reality. The
first question, then, is not "What is religion?" It is

rather "What is religion about? What are the universal religious facts of common human experience to which religious symbols refer?" I have suggested for your consideration that religion is about community; that the reference is to the need to overcome estrangement, reconcile those who are at enmity, and so re-establish the brotherhood of mankind, in the way in which Jesus revealed to us, which is the way of the Cross; and in reliance upon the guidance of the Spirit of God.

Undoubtedly the most significant indication of the change that is upon the Church is the movement for the reunion of the churches and other separate Christian fellowships. The ecumenical movement is itself a deep change in the outlook of Christians everywhere. We are reaching out to one another, recognizing our brotherhood in Christ and seeking to find an expression for it that will make us, and manifest that we are, one Church of Christ. The old antagonisms and enmities between sects are dying out. Friendship, sympathy and co-operation are increasing. This is the ecumenical movement. Can any Christian conscience fail to realize in it the work of the divine Spirit in his Church?

To further the movement towards reunion which is implicit in the ecumenical movement, various Councils have been set up throughout the world, including the British Council of Churches and the World Council of Churches. In the work of these organizations the Society of Friends has played its part ever since the Edinburgh Conference of 1910. These Councils are undoubtedly of first importance for the future of Christianity and, indeed, of religion in the world. For until the Church has overcome the differences within it and reconciled its own antagonisms, and done so openly and manifestly, how can it call upon the nations to be reconciled without being laughed out of court? The task of these Councils is to work patiently to overcome the differences that separate the Christian organizations and so make reunion possible. Surely, if we are to be true to our own Christian meaning and purpose we must continue and indeed increase our co-operation with the Councils with energy and enthusiasm.

There is a difficulty, however, which concerns the basis of membership of these Councils. The great majority of churches and religious bodies seek the basis in a declaration of doctrinal belief as simple as possible, provided that it defines them as indeed Christian bodies in a fashion acceptable to all. The Society of Friends, on the other hand, objects to any attempt to define membership of a Christian body in terms of beliefs, and has therefore found it impossible, up to date, to accept any such formulation as a basis which it might approve. Until recently, an exception was made in our favour by the British Council of Churches on the ground that we were among the original bodies who co-operated in setting up the Council. But last year the British Council of Churches adopted the basis agreed by the World Council, and this basis, which is still a doctrinal one, we are now invited to accept. If we still find ourselves unable to agree to such a basis, we have been offered Associate Membership, which will enable us to continue to play our part in the life and work of the British Council of Churches, with the proviso that we may not "take part in any vote on a proposal to amend the constitution".

To some of us it may seem right to make an exception to our internal practice for the sake of working in full membership with the other Christian bodies, in and through these Councils. It may indeed seem captious to refuse. My considered opinion is that this is not the case; rather, I believe, our continued refusal to accept a doctrinal basis of membership could be an important contribution to the success of the ecumenical movement. Let me explain why I think this.

When I was received into fellowship by the Society of Friends only a few years ago, I had no proper grasp of the spirit of the Quaker tradition. In my desire to be clearly aware of what I had committed myself to, I considered it of the first importance to decide what might be the central issue from which the character of Quakerism arises. What is it, I found myself asking, which differentiates the Society of Friends from the other separate fellowships into which the Christian Church has been broken up? The Society of Friends is one of the Christian sects. It is a sect with a difference. What precisely is this difference? I found this question difficult to answer until I noticed that the other sects were differentiated from one another by specific differences of doctrinal belief. But this mode of distinction could not be used in the case of Friends. Rather we are distinguished from all the other sects by an absence of definitive doctrinal beliefs[1]—indeed by an objection to them. This seemed to be the central issue for which I was seeking: but it needed a positive and not a merely negative formulation. The conclusion I reached

---

[1] By a "definitive doctrinal belief" I mean a doctrinal belief such that if I cannot assent to it, I exclude myself and ought to be excluded from the Society of Friends.

is this. The central conviction which distinguishes the Society of Friends is that Christianity cannot be defined in terms of doctrinal beliefs; that what makes us Christians is an attitude of mind and a way of life; and that these are compatible with wide variations and with changes in beliefs and opinions.

This has an important bearing upon the method whereby the reunion of the Christian bodies might be achieved. If our Christianity cannot be definitively expressed in doctrines to be accepted or, it would seem to follow, in particular forms of church organization or of worship, then it cannot be necessary that agreement on these must precede a union of the churches. The fact that they recognize one another as Christian is itself sufficient as a basis of unity. A joint public declaration that a member of any is, as of right, a member of all would be the first and the decisive step. Discussions of doctrine, of ritual and of organization could go on within the unity so achieved. It might indeed be discovered that the variety and difference, or much of it, that exists is of permanent value within the unity of the Church. If this Quaker standpoint were accepted by the other Christian bodies, reunion could take place tomorrow. I doubt whether it can be effectively achieved on other terms. Indeed I doubt whether uniformity in Christian belief or practice is itself desirable.

By rejecting any definitive doctrinal expression of its Christian faith, the Society of Friends undid the distortion of Christianity through the influence of Greek philosophy, at least to a considerable extent. The effect is to shift the expression of Christianity from theory to practice. "By their fruits ye shall know them" becomes the accepted rule. Faith no longer means the acceptance of an established creed or the assent to an authoritative system of doctrine. It recovers its original meaning of trust and fearless confidence; and this spirit of faith is expressed in a way of living which cares for one another and for the needs of all men. Our Christianity is a practical discipleship of Jesus in all the relationships of daily life. Our witness against slavery and war; our activities of social service at home and abroad are large-scale public manifestations of this spirit, by which the world judges the meaning and the character of our religion. To this we must add that the power which creates and renews this spirit in us and which inspires and directs this discipleship, we find in the quiet simplicity of our corporate worship of God. The experience of this way of life must have its own reflective aspect, but it will be rather a tentative and continuing search for a truth grounded in our experience than an effort to conform to a pattern of belief already guaranteed. For this reason we must, in sharing the effort towards reunion of the Church, insist upon this principle, as essential to Christianity and as the condition of a reunion which will not contain the seeds of its own disruption, and which will make possible the fulfilment of the task of the Church in the salvation of the world.

This overcoming of the theoretical bias of traditional Christianity amongst us is not, however, complete. The unreality of idealism and even of sentimentalism still, on occasion, distorts our worship. But more important is the individualism, which is an inevitable concomitant of the dualism which gives rise to the emphasis on theory and belief. In action we are in living contact with the world outside us; while for our spiritual or theoretical activities, we retire into ourselves, and into a world of ideas. This world in ourselves is an imaginary world, whose validity depends wholly upon a correct reference to the material world—the world in which we act. It is only in action that we meet anyone but ourselves; and it is only in meeting others that we find ourselves and our own reality. We are not individuals in our own right; and in ourselves we have no value at all, since we are meaningless. Our human Being *is* our relations to other human beings and our value lies in the quality of these relations. Our relation to God is itself real only as it shows itself in our relation to our neighbours. So the scriptures say, "If any man says he loves God, and loves not his brother, he is a liar; the truth is not in him." This is that "likeness" between the two great commandments of which Jesus spoke. Individualism, therefore, is an error. The truth is that we are human beings only by being members of a community.

I shall return to this issue in my conclusion. But first there are a few elements of our Quaker tradition which deserve to be mentioned. Our refusal to *define* our faith in doctrinal terms is essential. We are not Christians *because* we believe this or that. Yet this does not justify the rejection of theory altogether. It seems to me, rather, that we may be suffering in our witness from the lack of serious effort to find adequate theoretical expression for the implications of our religious activity and of our Christian discipleship. Holding fast to our refusal to *define* our faith in doctrinal terms, might we not create a new and acceptable kind of theology, which should be undogmatic; and which, like modern science, would recognize the hypothetical and temporary character of all its findings? Such an effort, as I see it, should proceed under certain presuppositions. It should be empirical in temper, checking theory against contemporary experience, religious and scientific. It should be freely critical of the past, recognizing that in this field of knowledge as in others, antiquity is no indication of validity. It should recognize that it is impossible to believe what one does not understand, and undesirable to profess to believe what one cannot believe effectively. It should be concerned to reject openly and explicitly what it can no longer accept, and it should not expect nor too eagerly desire unanimity. A competent group might begin with a critique of traditional theology; and if, as is likely, different viewpoints appear then a set of different "theologies" might be developed. This would have the advantage of showing how divergent views and doctrines could be held within a unity of love, and would avoid any tendency to produce final and definitive doctrines which could become binding, as an orthodoxy, upon the Society as a whole. Such an enterprise might, in itself, make an important contribution to the ecumenical movement, as well as educating the Society itself in the meaning of its own convictions.

The witness against slavery, in which we played a good part, is now in principle unnecessary, because of its success, though there are places where slavery still exists clandestinely. The witness against war is still with us, and must be vigorously carried on, though it, too, is nearing its term. For it is now accepted by the more developed nations that war is a senseless and futile method of settling disputes, and a practical organization has been set up, in the United Nations, to prevent and ultimately to eliminate it. Indeed, it seems likely that the pressure of events will compel the nations into some effective political union of the world. We should then find ourselves in a recurrence of the historic situation from which Christianity emerged, and facing the same problem that faced Jesus. The Church would be included in a world unity of political organization, maintained by power, just as the Jewish people found themselves part of the Roman Empire, protected by the Roman peace. Our question would be His question, "Is this the promised brotherhood of Man?" Our answer, like His, would have to be "No!" Our task would then be to transform it into the Kingdom of Heaven on earth.

I have expressed my conviction that the refusal of doctrinal definition is fundamental, not only to our Quaker faith, but also to the recovery, by the Church, of the reality of the Christian religion. I should like to add that the same is not true of our rejection of ritual. In the first place, there is a confusion here. All religious activities in the narrow sense—all activities of corporate worship, that is to say—are ritual activities. For they are reflective activities, which symbolize and refer to something beyond themselves. The communion which they achieve refers to a common life in the everyday world. The sense of unity which the assembly for worship generates in the worshippers refers to their practical unity in the daily life outside. If it does not, then it is merely sentimental and futile. The Quaker meeting for worship is, therefore, a ritual. It contrasts with the rituals of the churches by its extreme simplicity.

74

It has, for this reason, only a pragmatic justification. Its ritual symbolizes, in the barest and most direct fashion, that freedom and equality which together constitute the structure of friendship, and of all real personal relationship. I find this simplicity of symbolism both appealing and effective. Other Christians might find it too bare and unadorned for its symbolic purpose. It might be objected that it is *too* simple; that there are characters of the common life which ought to be represented in the symbolism of our worship but are not. Our rejection of the symbol of the common meal—the sacrament of Holy Communion—it might be said, impoverishes our ritual. For it leaves us with nothing to express our relation to Christ as members of His church; and also with no material reminder that though we do not live by bread alone, we can have no common life without it. I have no wish, in saying this, to suggest any change in our ritual of worship. I only wish to point out that it *is* a ritual; and that any change in it that seemed desirable could be accepted without a basic change in our religious witness, though the acceptance of a doctrinal definition of our basis of unity could not.

*   *   *   *   *

Here then we reach the term of this long discourse, and it remains only to summarize it. I have tried to express in it how I came to be profoundly dissatisfied with the Church as I found it and with the theological tradition in which I had been brought up. I have tried to explain the reasons for my dissatisfaction, and how they drove me into a life-long search for reality

6B

in religion—a search which led me to certain conclusions as to the nature of religion in general and of the Christian religion in particular. The search had from the beginning a practical objective, to eliminate war from human life. In its development, however, it has widened its scope and become more positive in its intention. It has become an effort to discover the task of the Christian Church in the twentieth century, and the conditions for undertaking and fulfilling that task. I can now summarize my conclusion in a few words with a good hope that you will understand it and the ground on which it rests. The task of the Church today, I believe, is what it always has been—to co-operate with God under the guidance of the Spirit of Christ in establishing on earth the Kingdom of Heaven. The means for accomplishing this task is the means that Jesus taught to His first disciples. The Church must be a real community on earth which exhibits to the world, in its life and in the relations of its members, the image of the Kingdom of Heaven, and which acts, in relation to the world outside, in the spirit of that Kingdom, by the way of the Cross.

I should like to end with this statement, for it is, for me, the conclusion of the whole matter, and complete in itself. But I fear for its interpretation, under the influence of the insidious idealism of our traditional thinking, and of the dualism which gives rise to it. To avoid this may I return to the consideration of our Quaker witness against war, and say a word about its implications? War is essentially a political act. To refuse to take part in war is to challenge the State on conscientious grounds. Now the State is an instrument for maintaining, modifying and enforcing law;

and law, in turn, is a means for achieving an effective co-operation of all citizens in their common life. To refuse to obey the law which demands that I take up arms in defence of my country, as being against my conscience, can only mean that for me war is a misuse of power. The basic question is about the uses and abuses of power by the State. Our refusal of war sets limits to the use of power, and therefore sets limits to the State, which, in the last resort, can only act by the exercise of power.

Now it is characteristic of the activity of Jesus in His relations with men, and of the mode of life He commended to His disciples, that power is set aside completely. "Not by might, nor by power, but by my spirit, saith the Lord." The reason is not that power is immoral, but that it is useless for the task ahead. The world cannot be saved by the exercise of power. Man must return to God freely of his own will, because only in this way can a real community of men arise. By power, in war, you strive to "impose your will upon the enemy"; and by power, in peace, you restrain the potential lawbreaker from acting against the law and force social co-operation upon him. To use power, in either case, is to appeal to fear: it is to make another afraid to refuse obedience to your command. The kingdoms of this world rest upon the appeal to fear, because they must take people as they are. But the Church of Christ, if it is to save the world, must *not* take men and women as they are; it must transform them, by using the only motive that can overcome fear, the power of love. And if it is to do this it must itself already have been transformed by love.

Again this is nothing ideal or virtuous or supernatural. Any real community—like any real family which is the analogue of all community—is a unity based on love. If the Church is to be a community which can transform the world, it must put aside the proclamation of law resting on fear in exchange for the insights of love; it must refuse to punish and instead forgive; and it must therefore refuse to defend itself, as its Master did, and in its defencelessness it must enter on the way of the Cross.

This is our clue to the proper relation between Church and State. The State acts through fear to maintain the common life of a society. The Church acts through love to maintain and to create a community. The task of the Church can only be carried out by religious means, never by political means. So the notion that State and Church can co-operate in saving the world is an illusion. The Kingdom of Heaven cannot be set up by the State. This is the meaning of Jesus saying, "My kingdom is not of this world; otherwise my servants would fight." Yet it is *in* this world that the Kingdom of Heaven must come.

If then we are to understand what it means for the Church to be a community in the world and in the world to create the community of mankind, then we must disabuse our minds of all notion of a partnership between Church and State; of the age-old influence of the doctrine of the two swords—the spiritual wielded by the Church, and the material sword wielded by the State. The Church has nothing to do with any sword, spiritual or material, nor has it any authority save the authority of love. The effect of the old dualist doctrine is to reduce the Church to playing a game of spiritual politics—and such politics are imaginary, or

78

if not they make the Church a rival of the State for secular power. The Church must do its whole task by itself. The State at most can make it easier or at least abstain from making it impossible. Freedom, equality and brotherhood are religious ends. To make them political objectives is to make sure of disillusion and disaster. The State is incapable of realizing them; its business is only with justice, so far as justice can be secured by law.

The final issue that we shall have to face will be concerned with the *economics* of the Kingdom of Heaven. It is obvious that the self-regarding and competitive nature of the co-operation by which we produce the means of life and distribute them amongst ourselves is wholly incompatible with the behaviour of a society based upon love and trust. If the Church is to be a real community in the world; if its Christianity is not to be defined in doctrines but expressed in action; and if its task is to manifest to the world the image of the Kingdom of Heaven then surely the manner and the spirit in which its members provide for one another's material needs must stand in strong and visible contrast with the attitudes and habits of the world around it. It will hardly be enough to prove that it cannot be produced by the compulsion of law and organization, by any form of socialist or communist power. We shall have to show it being achieved, across all national boundaries, by love and in freedom, in our own corporate life.

In the circumstances of His time, it seems, Jesus decided that this could only be achieved by embracing poverty. He is reported to have said that, humanly speaking, it is impossible for a rich man to enter the

Kingdom of Heaven. How it is to be done in the twentieth century, in a society which has been partly transformed by the working of the Christian leaven in it during the centuries, I do not know. It will take a long and detailed enquiry to discover. That we should discover it and take action is urgent. The Church is under judgment by the world as never before; and what is needed is a practical demonstration that will establish our *bona fides*. To think that the disparity of material resources between rich men and poor men need make no difference to their community or their communion is disingenuous. Beyond a certain point it makes both of these impossible. To believe it irrelevant to our fellowship as Christians is a clear case of the idealism which I have deplored. A community which is merely spiritual is imaginary. The Church may deceive itself about this, but the world will not. Here then, rather than in the field of doctrine or of ritual or of Church government, lies the major problem of the ecumenical movement. It cannot be solved by groups of Christians withdrawing into an artificial community-life which seeks to be materially self-supporting. The Church must remain fully in the world at its most contemporary. I see no reason why its members should not play their part in political life, or in the advancement of industry if they are so minded; nor why a corporate Christian body like our own should not use what influence it has for the defence or the extension of Christian principles in national or international life. But our main task is to become a *real* community in the world, and any effort to achieve this must aim from the beginning to be inclusive, to be both nternational and interdenominational. Its intention must be to unite all Christians throughout the world in a single brotherhood in which each cares for all in all their needs. This is a religious, not a political task, based not on self-interest or legal compulsion, but on love working in freedom.

This is as far as I can see. So I leave this final issue, with the others that I have raised, to your consideration and your judgment; and I do so in all humility, knowing how easy it is, in these great matters, to be mistaken.

SWARTHMORE LECTURES
PREVIOUS TO 1940

QUAKERISM: A RELIGION OF LIFE.
By RUFUS M. JONES, M.A., D.Litt.

SPIRITUAL GUIDANCE IN THE EXPERIENCE OF THE SOCIETY OF
FRIENDS. By WILLIAM C. BRAITHWAITE, B.A., LL.B.

THE COMMUNION OF LIFE.
By DR. JOAN M. FRY. Second Edition.

HUMAN PROGRESS AND THE INWARD LIGHT.
By THOMAS HODGKIN, D.C.L.

THE NATURE AND PURPOSE OF A CHRISTIAN SOCIETY.
By T. R. GLOVER, M.A. Fourth Impression.

SOCIAL SERVICE: ITS PLACE IN THE SOCIETY OF FRIENDS.
By JOSHUA ROWNTREE.

THE HISTORIC AND THE INWARD CHRIST.
By EDWARD GRUBB, M.A.

THE QUEST FOR TRUTH.
By SILVANUS P. THOMPSON, F.R.S. Third Edition.

THE MISSIONARY SPIRIT AND THE PRESENT OPPORTUNITY.
By HENRY T. HODGKIN, M.A., M.B.

THE DAY OF OUR VISITATION. By WILLIAM LITTLEBOY.

THE NEW SOCIAL OUTLOOK. By LUCY FRYER MORLAND, B.A.

SILENT WORSHIP: THE WAY OF WONDER.
By L. VIOLET (HODGKIN) HOLDSWORTH. Third Impression.

QUAKERISM AND THE FUTURE OF THE CHURCH.
By HERBERT G. WOOD, M.A.

THE NATURE AND AUTHORITY OF CONSCIENCE.
By RUFUS M. JONES, M.A., D.Litt.

THE LONG PILGRIMAGE: HUMAN PROGRESS IN THE LIGHT OF THE
CHRISTIAN HOPE. By T. EDMUND HARVEY, M.A.

RELIGION AND PUBLIC LIFE. By CARL HEATH.

PERSONAL RELIGION AND THE SERVICE OF HUMANITY.
By HELEN M. STURGE.

THE INNER LIGHT AND MODERN THOUGHT.
By GERALD K. HIBBERT, M.A., B.D. Second Impression.

THE QUAKER MINISTRY. By JOHN W. GRAHAM, M.A.

THE THINGS THAT ARE BEFORE US.
By A. NEAVE BRAYSHAW, B.A., LL.B.

CHRIST AND THE WORLD'S UNREST. By H. T. SILCOCK, M.A.

THE LIGHT OF CHRIST. By JOHN S. HOYLAND, M.A.

SCIENCE AND THE UNSEEN WORLD.
By ARTHUR STANLEY EDDINGTON, F.R.S. Sixth Impression.*

DEMOCRACY AND RELIGION: A STUDY IN QUAKERISM.
By DR. G. SCHULZE-GAEVERNITZ. Second Impression.

CREATIVE WORSHIP By HOWARD H. BRINTON, Ph.D. Second Impression.

EDUCATION AND THE SPIRIT OF MAN. By FRANCIS E. POLLARD, M.A.

UNEMPLOYMENT AND PLENTY.
By SHIPLEY N. BRAYSHAW, M.I.Mech.E. Third Impression.

CHRIST, YESTERDAY AND TO-DAY.
By George B. JEFFREY, F.R.S. Second Impression.

OUR RESPONSE TO GOD. By WILLIAM E. WILSON, B.D. Second Impression

TOWARDS A NEW MANNER OF LIVING.
By DR. HOWARD E. COLLIER. Second Impression.

RELIGION AND CULTURE. By CAROLINE C. GRAVESON, B.A.

DEMOCRATIC LEADERSHIP. By A. BARRAT BROWN, M.A.

THE TRUSTWORTHINESS OF RELIGIOUS EXPERIENCE.
By D. ELTON TRUEBLOOD, Ph.D. Second Impression.

*All Out of Print except where indicated by ***

GEORGE ALLEN AND UNWIN LTD

GEORGE ALLEN & UNWIN LTD
London: 40 Museum Street, W.C.1

Auckland: 24 Wyndham Street
Bombay: 15 Graham Road, Ballard Estate, Bombay 1
Buenos Aires: Escritorio 454-459, Florida 165
Calcutta: 17 Chittaranjan Avenue, Calcutta 13
Cape Town: 109 Long Street
Hong Kong: F1/12 Mirador Mansions, Kowloon
Ibadan: PO Box 62
Karachi: Karachi Chambers, McLeod Road
Madras: Mohan Mansions, 38c Mount Road, Madras 6
Mexico: Villalongin 32-10, Piso, Mexico 5, DF
Nairobi: PO Box 5436
New Delhi: 13-14 Asaf Ali Road, New Delhi 1
São Paulo: Avenida 9 de Julho 1138-Ap. 51
Singapore: 36c Princep Street, Singapore 7
Sydney, N.S.W.: Bradbury House, 55 York Street
Tokyo: 3 Kanda-Ogawamachi, 3-Chome
Toronto: 91 Wellington Street West